The Blood Cries Out!

Joe and Stephanie DeMott

"For we do not wrestle with flesh and blood but, against principalities, against powers, against rulers of the darkness of this age, against spiritual hosts of wickedness in the heavenly places Eph 6:12

Forward

As a Denver homicide detective, Joe DeMott had a commitment to seeing that justice was done. Joe's dedication and determination to get to the truth made him a formidable homicide detective whose commitment extended beyond his normal caseload of horrendous homicides. Joe believed that cold cases needed to be reviewed and reworked with a fresh set of eyes. This commitment to solving cold cases led to justice for victims and their families, who had waited years for answers. Joe was part of an elite homicide unit, and his stories of the team's work never fail to amaze me. It was an honor to work alongside these dedicated individuals for decades, especially Joe whose dedication and determination came from his commitment to God and his family.

Mitch Morrissey Denver District Attorney (2005-2017)
Coauthor of The Denver District Attorney's Office: A History of Crime in the Mile High City

This book is dedicated to all the warriors that do battle in all realms on this earth in day-to-day affairs. Not only the full-time ministry worker, but the everyday Christian that lives the life of a warrior for Christ. We fight the good fight of faith. This book is also dedicated to my wife, Stephanie and Children Joseph, David, AnnaMarie and Jesse. For all the nights they woke up and I was gone from being called out on a Homicide. Thanks to them for the part they played in my career and now in Stephanie and my ministry to marriages.

The "Blood Cries Out" is a story of how my wife, Stephanie and I have seen God work in the lives of a working cop. Stephanie became a Christian at age 9. I knew who God was but had no personal relationship. Being a cop was all I wanted. It was the most important thing in my life, including being more important than my family. As I look back there were many times that God protected me even in my selfishness. Stephanie would pray for me while I was at work. Just like most police wives it wasn't easy with the shift work and the court, when you should have been sleeping, and off duty work. You really don't see each other very much and it is lonely for the spouses. I know Stephanie prayed for me often and I can remember many times to prove it. Many names have been changed but the stories are real. Some of the events it is very easy to see how God was working in the situation, some not so much. We have learned in many years of ministry that many times you don't see what God was up to until years later. I will try and tell you what it is like from my eyes. What I saw, how I felt and how all of it affected me. How it affected my wife, my family, and the way we see ministry now.

Index

Chapter 1 –	Who Shapes Us	Pg 7
Chapter 2 –	Rookie	Pg 14
Chapter 3 –	Veteran Cop	Pg 17
Chapter 4 –	God on the Job	Pg 23
Chapter 5	Investigation 101	Pg 26
Chapter 6 –	Breaking a Curse	Pg 33
Chapter 7 –	The Mission	Pg 39
Chapter 8 –	Murder Pinned on Wrong man	Pg 45
Chapter 9 –	Mr. Homicide	Pg 48
Chapter 10 –	Spiritual Eyes	Pg 51
Chapter 11 –	Not him again	Pg 55
Chapter 12 –	Ready Set Go	Pg 57
Chapter 13 –	Still Small Voice	Pg 61
Chapter 14 –	Do Something, Something Happens	Pg 66
Chapter 15 –	The Abyss	Pg 68
Chapter 16 –	Lonely Days, Lonely Nights	Pg 71
Chapter 17 –	Dreams and Visions	Pg 77
Chapter 18 –	No Way	Pg 80
Chapter 19 –	The Beginning of the End	Pg 85
Chapter 20 –	Whirlwind	Pg 91

Chapter One – Who shapes us?

I was hired by the Denver Police Department as a Cadet right out of high school and started the job on August 16th, 1973. I was just starting to date Stephanie, the woman I would marry. We were both very young. I was 18 and she was 17. We thought we knew what love was but did not understand commitment. She was a Christian and I was from a religious home, but I did not have a personal relationship with Jesus. Our relationship was headed for trouble from the very beginning. I was beginning to be more controlling and jealous. The environment of the police department at that time was very stressful. One of the first assignments I had was working at the front desk at headquarters which then was at 1331 Champa St. The building was built in 1939 and plans for a new building were underway. The city jail was on the 4th floor of the building. This is where all arrests were brought to be booked, fingerprinted and jailed until court, or bailed out or transferred to the county jail.

One night when I came to work, I was confronted by one of the officers that I worked with at the Desk. He had been on the job for many years. On this night he had been drinking and came to work drunk. We were in the back room where the records room was. The officer and I did not know each other very well as I was a very new Cadet. I remember I used to admire this officers Smith and Wesson 38 revolver because it had an unusual pistol grip. There was a thumb rest on it. I never saw that anywhere else. Suddenly, he pulled his pistol and shoved it in my ribs and pushed me against the wall. I could smell the alcohol on his breath. To this day I couldn't tell you what he said or if he said anything, but I thought I was going to die right there. I kind of figured out with the veiled threat what the message was, and I kept my mouth shut about his intoxication. I never admired that pistol grip again.

I had many experiences working on the desk. Some officers would come by the desk and just pepper spray us Cadets. I guess to see if we could handle it. I guess it was part of our initiation into a whole new world. I had no idea. At the same time frame the Denver Police Department was at war with a subversive organization that was putting bombs around town and had shoot outs with Denver Officers. Officers had been wounded in these gunfights. Because of this the front desk at HQ was built across the entire front entrance. No one was allowed in the building unless they had been cleared by one of the officers. There was a men's restroom right as you came through security. One night a bomb was discovered in that bathroom. Someone had placed a bomb in one of the stalls. I had been in that bathroom at the same time. It was set up to detonate if someone opened the door of the stall. Detective Steve Tanberg, of the Robbery Unit, and I searched every floor of the building looking for suspicious packages or a person that had slipped by security. Nothing or no one was found. Looking back this was the second time God had saved my life.

There were many funny times I remember also. I remember working in the Identification Bureau. There was a group of Officers working there that were a bunch of comedians! They would pick on this one Cadet all the time. One day one of the Techs grabbed that Cadet and hung him upside down out the window. That was scary. One of the more harmless events was the Tech that used to use fingerprint ink for his pranks. In the old days many restrooms had toilets with black seats. Yes, you guessed it. Fingerprint ink on the toilet seat made a great impression.

Stephanie and I were married on August 11, 1975, when I was still a Cadet. As a Cadet we had the privilege to go to college on a LEA Grant, Law Enforcement Association. If our grades were a B average, we had the opportunity to ride twice a month on patrol with officers. It was a great reason to keep the grades up. We went to Metropolitan College in Downtown Denver. Used to say "MIT". Not that one "Massachusetts Institute of Technology" but "Metro in town." I mostly rode on the morning shift in District 2 with Officer Rick Baker. Baker was a funny guy, and a great cop. He liked to stay very busy and would teach as we worked. I liked the morning shift, 3 am to 11 am. In District 2 it was very busy for the first part of the shift. But the draw was they were all solo cars. So, I got to ride in the front seat. The night shift cars were all two-man cars.

I met many officers working as a Cadet. One of the other District two officers that really impressed me was Don DeBruno. He was a husky muscular Italian guy that had a sense of humor that could deescalate any situation. A nice Italian boy. He and Rick Baker were good friends. Don was promoted to detective and eventually was assigned to the Homicide Unit. Hence the first seed planted for me to want to work Homicide. In the early morning hours on December 10, 1975, Stephanie and I faced our first tragedy of an officer, I knew well and admired, being killed. Stephanie and I were alerted to it in such a strange way that when we think of it to this day it is very chilling. We were asleep and suddenly, our clock radio, which was popular in 1975, turned on and we heard the unfortunate news, a Denver Police officer had been killed. The alarm was not set to go off or was it close to the time to go off. The officer was a Homicide Detective, Don DeBruno. Don and other Detectives were attempting to arrest a fugitive from Canada wanted for murder. Don was shot and killed while he and his partner attempted to serve warrants on a man wanted for six thefts in Kentucky. The suspect was also wanted for the murder of a man in Toronto, Canada. Detective DeBruno and his partner located the man at the Denver Bus Station. A gunfight ensued. Don was shot in the chest, his partner, Detective Dave Haley, was wounded. In the blazing gunfire that ensued the suspect was critically wounded. The suspect, 29, was shot four times and was paralyzed from the waist down. He was sentenced to life in prison but became eligible for parole in 2006. His parole was denied. He had another hearing in December 2007 that was denied. The suspect died in prison in 2013.

We were very shaken up the night the radio went off. Stephanie realized on that day how dangerous the job was as it was brought home in a personal way. Stephanie was fearful of me being killed. She did not want me to be a police officer. For me it gave me more determination to go out on the streets and fight crime.

I finally started at the Police Academy on April 1, 1976. Boy what an April Fool's joke that was on the DPD. There was a constant fear among Cadets that we would not get hired as actual officers. There was another Cadet with me in the Academy. Another Cadet and I had not turned 21 yet. We went through the entire class not knowing for sure if we would get hired as official sworn officers.

I remember I would come home and try my newly learned arrest tactics on Stephanie, it was not appreciated. We were a young married couple living in a nice apartment. One time I had a poker game at our apartment with some of the other recruits from the academy. They had real guns because they were sworn officers. Everyone was passing around their revolvers with a sense of excitement. At this time, we weren't allowed automatics yet. They were all admiring each other's guns. There were 4-inch barreled Colt Pythons and 4-inch Smith and Wesson 38's. Some were .357 Magnums. We weren't allowed to carry .357 rounds. But .38's can be used in the .357 revolvers. Some were blue and some were nickel plated. Boy we were all impressed. Those Colt Pythons had a ribbed barrel on the top and were ominous looking. I preferred the Smith and Wesson model 19 .357 Magnum which felt the best in my hand. I carried a blue 4-inch model 19 for a couple of months. I then bought a 6-inch nickel plated 19. I went on to carry this gun in the detective bureau for years. After all Dirty Harry carried a Smith. During the poker game these guys, me included, were ordering Stephanie around asking for drinks, dips and chips. Stephanie became very irritated with being treated like a maid and showed her ingenuity. She took a full bag of unopened Dorito chips from the kitchen and smashed it which caused a loud gunshot sound. Gotta, admit it got everyone's attention as they jumped off their seats and Stephanie snickered thinking "I'm not your maid". Knowing Stephanie's gentle temperament this was very unusual behavior.

I was very influenced by what I saw on television and the movies. The danger and excitement intrigued me. For three years I worked as a cadet and went to college majoring in Police Science.

From the very beginning I was hoping and politicking to be assigned to District Two. I remember going to district two station and having a sit down with Captain Pennel. I met him while I was a Cadet. If I remember right, I pretty much begged him to get me assigned to his District. At that time in the 70's District Two was the northeast part of Denver. It was the busiest and roughest part of the city. To be a cop in Denver you must be 21. Since I was allowed to start the academy on April 1st of 1976, I went through the entire academy as a Cadet turning 21 in June and the class was graduating at the end of July. I officially was sworn in on August 1st. I remember when the class was over. I was told to put my Cadet Uniform on and report to District Two. I was to work at the desk until August 1st when I would be sworn in officially. Sorry to say but I could not imagine wearing that grey shirted uniform instead of the blue police uniform. I lied and said I had burnt my Cadet Uniform. So, I took the week off and reported as a full fledge Denver Police Officer.

Once you hit the street you are assigned a training officer. Probation lasted a year. It was decided as time went on how long you had to be with a Training Officer. My first Training Officer was a real character. Graham Haney was a guy that could be charming and un-assuming or whatever he had to be for the situation, what a guy. He chewed on a cigar sometimes right down to a nub. We were working the day shift out in the eastern part of the district called Montebello in August 1976. It was very hot and although guys just started wearing bullet proof vests sometimes I didn't. I remember how I felt driving in a police car as a real live official cop. The memories of the three years as a Cadet just faded away. Now I was carrying a gun and wearing a badge. Denver's badge is distinctive. There is an Eagle on the top with the city of Denver seal in the middle. There are seven points that represent the seven virtues: Honesty, Temperance, Faith, Charity, Hope, Fortitude and Integrity. To me it represented something very meaningful.

The Montebello area was not very busy. We had a lot of burglary reports to make and a lot of construction sites to check. We spent a lot of time at the firehouse with the fireman. I remember that we would have poker games with the firemen that were on duty. There was a rule that if a call came out and one or both of us had to leave, we had to put the cards face down. We would continue that hand when we came back after the call. This was a very well-known rule, and everybody adhered to it.

I do Remember one day that we were having a poker game with about 10 people. There was Graham Haney and I from the Police Department and the rest were firemen. The alarm went off for a fire call. All the firemen jumped up to get their gear. Everyone put their cards down on the table and Graham Haney and I jumped up to cover the fire department on their call. The fire call was basically a false alarm. The fire department was not needed so all of us went back to the Firehouse. We resumed our places in front of our cards. As we sat at the poker table, we realized that all the cards had been put back in the deck. The fire captain said that he had "changed the rules", and he had put all the cards back on the deck. If I remember right that was the last time that I personally played cards with the fire department. Most of our time was spent just patrolling the streets, as I said, Montebello was a quiet neighborhood at the time. No doughnuts LOL.

Chapter Two – Rookie

Towards the end of August during my training time with Graham Haney we received a call at an apartment house. We got a call of a man with a gun threatening suicide in his apartment off Elmendorf Pl. Sometimes these calls are someone wanting you to see them with a gun and doing the job for them, "suicide by cop". The apartment building was white, and the entrance to the apartments was outside. We went up to the door of the location. We knocked on the door and were mindfully ready for anything. Well maybe not everything. The guy that opened the door was holding a snub nosed 38 cal. Pistol to his head. We weren't ready for this. I guess we both had the same idea because Graham and I both went for him instead of our guns. The guy had cocked the weapon. A 2-inch stainless-steel snub-nosed revolver. I put my right thumb between the hammer and the frame, the fight was on. The two of us had a real battle with this guy to get that gun away and get him handcuffed. Turned out the guy was an ex-cop from Texas. He had lost his family in a divorce. He was very distraught. I remember sweating and being very worn out from the fight. The adrenaline makes your heartbeat fast, you shake, and you wonder, what if? Graham and I were both put in for the Medal of Honor. We didn't get it because I was a rookie. That's what Haney was told. One of my first experiences of weird excuses. I think Haney was also upset. He wore a previous Medal of Honor on his uniform, so he wasn't as upset. No matter what job you have you're going to have situations where silly decisions are made. The problem is everyone that makes these decisions is human. Humans are driven by their personal experiences, their personal prejudices and their jealousies. To be honest it took my whole 30-year career and many years of retirement to finally put many of these things aside and not think about them anymore.

The next month I was working with a bigger character, Terry Walton. He also was a training Officer on the day shift. He was one of the original District Two "Wild Horse Riders". In other words, anything goes! These guys were mean and tough. He wouldn't let me drive the police car for a long time. Guess he wanted to remind me that I was just a rookie. Walton was one of those guys that could really degrade you. He made you feel very small. I'm not sure what his motivation for that was but it did toughen you up. One day he took my police hat and crushed it. In those days we were forced to wear our hats whenever we got out of the police car. We were required to wear it whether it was a traffic stop or a call for help or to go into a home to make a report. A lot of guys didn't like to do that because it was cumbersome to wear that hat. The hat was very uncomfortable. That poor hat looked terrible; I didn't know how I was going to explain that to the sergeant the next day at roll call. In some ways that was funny. In other ways it was degrading. I was able to uncrumple it, so it looked presentable. How long is this going to last??? Will my next training officer be like this? Wish I knew about forgiveness at this time it would have made life a lot easier.

When I worked with Walton, we worked in sector 2 of District 2 which was further West in the District than Montebello and busier, more crime. It was also a Colfax car which was a very busy part of town. As I said Walton would not let me drive the car for many weeks after I started to work with him. It got to be very irritating and boring for me as it was an awesome thing to be driving a police car deciding where to patrol and what to do as a rookie cop. I decided to confront and challenge Walton about the fact that I wanted to drive during our patrol. One day I told him that I had already totaled a police car when I was a cadet so what was the big deal? Walton looked at me and threw me the keys. What a great feeling, now I'm in control! That's what I thought anyway.

One afternoon we were on patrol and made a simple traffic stop and he let me go up to the car by myself. I still can see Terry's boot tip on the car console as he kicked back and watched me. I remember asking the man to step to the curb. I looked at his right hand and saw a small semi-automatic pistol cradled in his hand. I immediately hit the weapon out of his hand and got the cuffs on him pronto. That day I gained my training officer's respect. All I know now is God's grace was there for me.

Before I became a Christian in 1983, police work was just bad guys and good guys. You could feel the evil in people. Or least you thought it was in them. Then of course cops were hard as rocks themselves. They didn't know they were hard they just thought it was normal to harden their hearts. It is easy for the seasoned veteran police officer that sees the day-to-day tragedies of life in the big city to become calloused. They also develop a dark sense of humor. I was one of them until Jesus Christ came into my life and softened my heart. Not only to Him but to people of all races and Nationalities. Now I see everything differently. All people are Gods children and are equals. The bible says the heart is deceitful so anyone can be evil without God.

Chapter 3 – Veteran Street Cop

I worked the street as a patrolman for 7 ½ years in the worst part of town before becoming a detective. We made sometimes 3 times the Felony Arrests a month more than the next team in the district. I had a reputation of "always getting my man". I remember one of my Sergeants telling me that there were two kinds of mistakes, one of the mind, and one of the heart. Before meeting Jesus Christ, I made plenty of both. The street criminals called me "Cigar" because I always had a Nicaugarian Jose Melende cigar in my mouth. Eventually everyone in the district called me "Cigar." They were expensive cigars and required a humidor. The name caught on and everyone called me that even to this day. I tried to be fair to people. There were different kinds of criminals. Some were not as harmful as others. I promised myself that if I could help it, I would do everything I could to be the one going home after the shift was over. I thought I was so tough. My partner and I would walk into a tough bar called the "EDI" the East Denver Inn. The bartender would turn down the music so I could use the phone to call in ID checks. They would put on a song called "He's so tough". I was a real "legend in my own mind". The cigar was part of the legend.

During my time on the street my wife Stephanie was trying to hold the family together. The first seven or so years I worked on the street she would pray for me. As I said before she became a Christian at an early age. I remember one night when my partner, Jim Ward, and I were on patrol in one of the worst parts of town at that time. The Precinct number was 214. I loved being assigned to the area and working with Jim every night. Jim and I got to know each other very well. The area was from Broadway to Washington St, and Colfax Ave to 20th Ave. The area consisted of many bars and apartment buildings as well as office buildings. Most of the buildings were old, over 50 to 80 years old. It was a very racially diverse area and many of the bars were gay bars and the shops porno shops. Our routine was one arrest, a moving citation and 5 parking tickets before coffee. We had more radio calls than any car in the city every month. Man, it was good.

Jim Ward was a great cop. He could tell when someone was lying to us and got them to fess up. He also ran like a cheetah. This was crazy because he smoked like a chimney. He would stick his cigarette in his mouth and take off after guys. He would always catch them. He was a Navy Veteran and was a fireman on a ship during Vietnam. There was a breakout of arson for about a month fire in our area, almost every night. One night we drove up to an apartment house on fire and called it in on the radio. Before I knew it Jim had run into the fire because people were yelling there were people inside. I tried to follow him in remembering what he had told me about staying low. I got maybe 50 feet in and had to run back out. I could not handle the smoke. I felt like a coward after that night. I also felt bad that I let Jim down. He was ok that I couldn't do it. He saved someone that night and was given a medal.

One night at about midnight. We drove through the alley watching the drug deals and pimps. Jim spotted a guy that looked suspicious. I was driving and stopped the car just as we were pulling into the street from an alley. Jim hadn't gotten out of the police car but saw something in the man's back pocket. Jim tried to grab for the object and before he could the man pulled it out. He pointed a revolver right at my partner's stomach. We both grabbed the gun and began to fight over the weapon. I jumped out of the car and ran around to grab him. No one was hurt. There was no time to think, just react. When I went home that night Stephanie told me she had been awoken from her sleep. She had a very bad feeling and started to pray for me right at the same time this happened. My friend that is how God works. Even though at the time I was very far from God. At that time, I was not very thankful and did not really understand what had happened spiritually.

Jim Ward and I would park the car and walk the beat in those days. Most didn't but we loved it. It allowed us to be able to talk to more people. We could see and hear things you can't while driving in a car. One night we received a call on a man with a gun near 20th and Broadway. Jim was driving and we saw a guy walking on 20th Ave east of Broadway. I jumped out of the car which was a 1978 Ford Crown Victoria. Jim quickly jumped out of the car also. Together we grabbed the guy and got the gun from him. We got him handcuffed, supercops! As we finished handcuffing him, we noticed our vehicle driving away east on 20th Ave. I took off after it. I was able to open the driver's door and get in. I stopped it just as it turned to go south the wrong way down Lincoln St.

During our time working together we were assigned to a special assignment in Sector 3. There had been a rash of Burglaries and our Sergent was assigned the task to stop them. So, Jim and I worked in the area. During this time there was a Homicide at 1670 Poplar St. on December 7th, 1978. It was a very tragic case where a young mother, Madeleine Furey-Livaudais, had been brutally stabbed and raped while her husband was at work. Their two children, a boy and a girl were swinging in their baby swings. There were no suspects. We went door to door talking to neighbors and anyone who could help. No suspects were found.

I had worked with Ward for about 4 years when Jim decided he wanted to go the detective bureau. When Jim went to the Detective Bureau, I got to choose my new partner, Tony Eaton. He and I were Cadets together in the same academy class. He also liked walking the beat like I did. We would park our car and just walk up and down East Colfax Ave in the alleys. We would catch guys off guard. I used to twirl my night stick with its leather strap and bounce it off the ground. Boy, I thought I was cool. A regular "Blue Knight". Working on the street was exciting. It really is hard to explain. The down time was good as Tony, and I could talk about all different things, home and family. I loved working the night shift. We started at 7 pm and got off at 3 am. We were expected to be in the station by 3 am so the next shift could have the car. We very seldom were on time as we always took calls at the end of the shift when no one else would.

Before we got on the street we had roll call. The odd number Precincts came on at 6 pm and the even number precents came on at 7 pm. That way the city could be covered. Tony had started chewing tabaco. I of course had to follow and start chewing also. The next shift would complain because there was chew running down the outside of the patrol car right down over the badge. It caught on and others started to chew. One night during roll call you could hear a gulp. Someone swallowed their chew and the next thing you knew you heard others swallow theirs out of gag reaction. I quit. I didn't need it I had my cigar and my legend.

There was a bar on Colfax and Pearl St called the "Colony" at 569 E Colfax Ave. Nasty little places but great for catching bad guys. We used to say that working Colfax was like having a free ticket to the greatest show on earth. There was one guy that used to roller skate down the street wearing a pink tutu. Another guy had a python wrapped around his neck. Prostitutes everywhere. The Colony also turned the music down for us so we could collect ID's. We would call them in on the pay phone for any warrants. We would get all kinds of arrests from people wanted for dope and rape to killers. For real. You would walk in and at least half the people at the bar had felony records. I think about it today and don't know how we weren't afraid to go in there more than once a night and cause them trouble.

One day while I was still sleeping, I got a phone call from an Assault Detail Detective that wanted to see me. I went down to headquarters during the day to see what was up. Detective Garrison was a guy that had been on the job a long time. He told me that they had gotten information that a guy by the name of John Dixon wanted me dead. Apparently, he thought the pressure we put on the Colony Bar was ruining his criminal enterprise. I knew John Dixon very well. He was a black male about 6'6" and all muscle. Supposedly he almost played pro Baseball but decided to mess that up with drugs. The information was coming out of the County Jail and looked like good information. I remembered an incident in the past when my partner and I tried to arrest Dixon for some minor offense, He decided he didn't want to go to jail. All he had to do was lift us up off the ground as we each held on to one of his massive arms. We fought and fought and could not get his arms behind his back. Consequently, we dangled from his massive arms like rag dolls. Both of us shot mace up his nose and that just made him madder, and stronger.

As word got around about this threat against me people were concerned. The Sergeant I worked for told me to watch as I went home at night and make sure no one was following me. I did what he said. If I saw any headlights in my rear-view mirror as I left the police station, I would go home a different way or try to lose the car. Any way the rumors got worse. One night I called home and couldn't get an answer. Before cell phones you would just hope you could call in between calls and reports. I called a neighbor, and they said it looked a little unusual at our house and there were kid's toys out on the porch. At the time we had three small kids. Stephanie would not normally leave stuff out like that. I told the Sergeant, Tom Haney, what was going on and he suggested that he take me home and we check it out. Everything was fine and my wife and kids had just gone to church with her sister. Man, I got to tell you I was scared. Haney said that if there were any more rumors, he was going to take me off car 214 and hide me somewhere. That scared me worse. I loved working in that precinct, it was the busiest in the city. And I loved the action. Something needed to happen. Haney was a Homicide Detective before he became a Sergeant and always talked about it, and I think that planted a lot of seed for me to do the same.

Chapter Four – God on the Job

One night we did a check on the Colony and made our usual appearance. As Tony and I left and drove north down the alley in the 1500 block of Pearl St. and Washington St. a shot rang out. We always drove with our windows open so we could hear the streets and what was going on. A bullet came whizzing through the passenger window and out the driver's window. We both looked toward the sound of the shot and somehow saw a flash. I was driving and we drove around looking for whoever fired the shot. We could not find anyone. We did not call the incident in on the radio. We knew for sure I would be taken off 214 and hidden away somewhere.
So, we kept our mouths shut. Boy, I loved working in that area. Anyway, the next day we heard that someone sent flowers (black roses) to the information desk at Downtown Headquarters in remembrance of "Cigar". Then that night we heard from several folks that a guy named Virgil Tyson was the shooter. He had told people he shot me. I had had a few run-ins with Tyson also. I knew he was an associate of Dixon's.

Before this happened, I always thought when people said they heard a bullet whizzing by, they were exaggerating! Well now I know they were right. I continued to watch every night to see if I was being followed. I continued to drive around on the way home just in case. Stephanie kept the kids in the house and was watchful. The whole situation was surreal and made her feel numb. Stephanie had a hard time processing the feelings and thinking that this was her life. She felt trapped and was careful not to let the kids be affected by it. She prayed to God for safety for all of us.

We put more pressure on the Colony and continued to go in and do ID checks and arrest people. Tony and I continued to hear that Virgil Tyson was the guy that shot at us.

A few weeks down the road Tyson was found stabbed to death in 5 points by a couple guys that he tried to rip off. Five Points at that time was a place near downtown Denver where 5 corners came together. In its heyday there were a lot a jazz clubs and Gambling Joints. One of our favorite places on the points was Zonas Hot Links. Now that was good eating! Never heard if there were any arrests made in the killing of Tyson...

I really struggled with the idea of leaving the street and going to the Detective Bureau. I really loved the streets, especially at night. You really felt like you were the good guy against evil. You also felt that you were the only protection for the people that could not protect themselves. There were many times that I could see God really was involved. One time there was a guy that we knew well that was threatening to kill himself with a knife. When we got to his apartment he was standing outside with the knife and would not drop it. His eyes were just dead. You could tell he meant business. We tried to get close, and he would just get more aggravated. Most people think that knives are not that dangerous and do not understand why cops shoot people with knives. A guy with a knife can generally run up on you and stab you before you can draw your weapon. I took my night stick and swung it with the leather tong and knocked the knife out of his hand. I was proud of myself, again a "legend in my own mind". God again protected me, and it took many more months to figure it out.

Reflecting on an incident involving knives when I was on the morning shift. I answered a call about a disturbance around 4 am. We worked solo cars on the morning shift. Sometimes it was very lonely on the shift. Sometimes you were so tired you could barely stand it. Between working off duty and going to court it felt like you never slept. Another officer covered me on this call, a big Hawaiian guy. We were in an old apartment house with dimly lit hallways. There was a smell that I cannot describe but remember it well. A guy came to the door and as soon as he opened the door, he came at me with a knife. He knocked me to the ground as I held the hand with the knife for dear life. Don't ask what the other officer was doing because to this day I only know one thing, nothing!!!

This guy with the knife was about 30 years older than me and strong as an Ox. You would not have even been worried if you saw the guy on the street very harmless looking. Unless he is coming at you with a knife with fire in his eyes!!! I realized later in my career that some of these people were just plain possessed of the devil. An evil force gave them this superhuman strength. I finally got the knife away and got him handcuffed. No reason for his actions. I am sure my wifes prayers again kept me safe.

Chapter Five - Investigations 101

Just before the summer of 1983 my marriage started to crumble. It started off on the wrong footing in the beginning and just got worse. I realized that my marriage could soon be over, and I was devastated. As I had said before Stephanie was a Christian and I was not. The bible tells us to not be unequally yoked with a non-believer.

You can get our testimony Booklet "Redemption" A story of a healed marriage" on Amazon or wherever.

I asked Jesus to heal my marriage and save my soul. It was a real experience where I really accepted Jesus as my Lord and Savior. I figured at that point maybe if I was home at night for the most part my marriage could survive. So, I started the process of becoming a Detective. For months after this I had to discover what being a Christian was. No cheap Grace! It was spiritual warfare, discipline and much faith. I had to search the bible for the answers.

I decided when I became a detective that I wanted to go after the worst criminals, killers. Those seeds were planted by what happened to Don DeBruno. The seeds that had been instilled through Tom Haney had started to grow. I found that not all victims of Homicide are innocent. Some victims put themselves in the position to be killed. They are involved when they lose their life to the drug dealer, gang banger or pimp. But it is obvious that most victims only have the police to speak for them. Not their family or friends, and in the crime of murder that is double fold.

I remember going into an interview for promotion to detective. The interview was with three Captains, all that I knew. Captain Doug White of the Crimes Against Persons Bureau had been my Sergeant on the morning shift in District 2 years before. Captain Daryl Bolton of the Narcotics Unit and Captain Chuck Ferguson of the Crimes Against Property Bureau were the interviewers. It was stressful. First, you wanted to make a good impression on all of them. Of course, so they would pick you. At the same time, I had no desire to work Narcotics or Crimes Against Property. I was outspoken that I wanted to work Homicide. They kind of laughed me off. I got picked but went right to Auto Theft which I didn't want at all. But at least I made it.

When I became a Christian about 9 months before leaving the street. I didn't know much about spiritual warfare. In the years to come I would learn many things about spiritual warfare. The devil is an evil entity but can not make a person do anything. They have free will. Only we as humans with our own free will make the choice to do the things we do, right or wrong.

"We wrestle not with flesh and blood, but against principalities, against powers, against the rulers of the darkness of this world, against spiritual wickedness in high places"

When I first became a detective, everyone knew I wanted to work in Homicide. After a year in Auto Theft and another year in the Assault Unit I was ready. I had just come through a rough time in my marriage. I had seen God heal my marriage. I was ready to see God move in my job. In 1986 I was told that I would not get into Homicide because of the trouble I previously had in my marriage. It was probably because people thought I was unstable. If they had known the truth, they would have known how messed up I really was before Christ. I became a Christian because of the trouble in my marriage. I believed God for the healing of my marriage for 2½ years. During that time was when I was promoted to Detective. So, for some I was way out there. Funny the Sergeant that told me "I wouldn't hold my breath waiting to go to Homicide" is today a Christian himself. So, I just continued to pray. Not long after, in March of 1986 I was transferred to Homicide. I would spend the next 11 years there. I began to see God move mightily in my wife Stephanie's life as well as mine.

God began to teach us how to pray together. We sought God for all things including police work. In my walk of faith, I learned the true evil of this world. We learned about the spiritual realm. It was amazing to learn how to live on the edge of both. Stephanie and I became very active in our church. We also became involved in a marriage ministry that taught us about our One Flesh and Covenant. We started to teach others and to this day minister to marriage all over the world.

The Homicide Unit is considered one of the most prestigious jobs in the police department and egos show it. It only makes sense that the best detectives should be in that assignment. For the most part that's the case. It is amazing how so many people believe in the spiritual realm but don't understand the good and evil in it all. As soon as I started in the unit, I started seeing God in it all. I began looking at old cases and asked God to help me solve them. My wife and I prayed for divine intervention in all my cases. We saw many miracles happen. Some called us Mr. and Mrs. Colombo and others just thought it was funny or crazy.

Many will not believe the stories in this book. Whether you are a believer in God or not trust me these stories are true. Some of the names of course will be changed. I hope it will bring understanding to some and faith to others. God is really in control. He wants to be part of your life, no matter who you are or your circumstance.

I was very vocal in my beliefs. I had a telephone receiver with a cord on it leading nowhere hanging from my wall by my desk. There was a sign next to it that said, "Prayer Line". It was a great feeling that I had a line to God. All I had to do was get on the phone. Of course, this phone line was just metaphoric visual. I also had a quote from a Famous New York Homicide Detective Lieutenant Vernon Geberth on my wall:

"Homicide Investigation is a profound duty. As an officer entrusted with such a duty, it is incumbent upon you to follow the course of events and the facts, as they are developed to their conclusion. Death Investigations constitutes a heavy responsibility, as such, let no person deter you from the truth nor your personal conviction to see that justice is done. Not only for the deceased, but for the surviving family as well. <u>And Remember</u>; You're working for God".

Before I was transferred to Homicide I was assisting in a case where there was a serial rapist. The rapes were occurring in the Capitol Hill area.

In March of 1986 a woman named Maureen McNaulty was strangled and sexually assaulted in her Capitol Hill Apartment. Everyone just assumed that finally this guy went too far and killed someone.

I hate watching police shows on TV. Especially the ones that every week they solve the case by finding forensic evidence. Many times, in weird places. Of course, in my day they couldn't do a lot of what they could do today but still, give me a break.

On this case though the crime lab came up with a lone fingerprint belonging to a Nelson Stubblefield 26 AKA as "Stallion".

The search was on! We had gotten information that "Stallion" had stereo equipment from the victim and was trying to sell it. Lieutenant Dave Michaud had the suspect's phone number. This is one of those things you never forget. We had the location surrounded. Sergeant Tom Haney had been back in Homicide as the supervisor. He now was being promoted to Lieutenant. He soon would be going to Internal Affairs. He was obviously glad to be working on this kind of case as a last hurrah, for now.

Michaud got on a pay phone about two blocks away and called "Stallion". Michaud went into his best gang banger voice and got "Stallion" to admit to having the stereo. At the same time Haney and I were kicking in the front door. We could hear "Stallion" telling Michaud "I gotta go the cops are at the door". And yes, we were. Haney and I knocked down the door and jumped him and cuffed him before he knew what hit him.

Haney was one of the best when it came to interrogating killers. I learned a lot from him. His reputation years later caused him to be involved in the Boulder Colorado murder case of Jon Benet Ramsey. He was asked to interview Patsy Ramsey, the mom of the little girl Jon Benet. That case has never been resolved.

Sgt. Haney was at HQ getting ready to interview Stallion. While this is happening at HQ we are still out on the street on the hunt. It's getting late now, and night had fallen. We had no idea where the second suspect, Jessie Phifer, was to be found. Several Detectives were out on the street just trying to find Phifer. I was with Detective Kenny Chavez who I broke in when he and I were on the street. We just decided to start talking to people and seeing if anyone knew this guy. We saw a car driving down the street. This is a moment I can say it had to be God. Looking suspicious we decided to stop it. We asked the driver if he knew Phifer. He said yes that he had just come from a poker game a couple blocks away. Phifer was there playing poker. Now you can say that is just great police work. Really? God is amazing is what I say.

We set up a plan. The house was on a corner and had a porch. The guy we talked to would agree to go to the poker game and see if Phifer was still there. If he was, the guy he would come back on the porch and light a cigarette. We would move in. Just like on TV.

So, we surrounded the house and Detective Armedia Gordon and Detective Mike Fiori were watching the front. Chavez and I were in the back. Sure, enough out comes the guy. He lights a cigarette and Armedia can't even believe it. She froze for a minute in amazement. She finally tells us on the radio, "he lit the cigarette". We all moved in. We walked right in the front door, and I walked up to Phiffer as he was sitting at the poker table with several other black males. I put my 6-inch Nickle Plated Smith and Wesson 357 Mag up to the back of his neck. "Don't move Jessie, you're under arrest". Would have made a great movie scene

Sgt Haney is interrogating Phiffer in the interview room. After Haney gets Phifer's verbal statement he starts the video. Phiffer starts to take off the necklace that he is wearing. Haney knew it belonged to the victim. Haney says, "no hold on we will get that later." Haney wants Phifer wearing the necklace to be caught on video. That's the difference between a good interviewer and an excellent interviewer. Another chilling time during an interview caught on tape.

Their story was that they did not mean to kill McNulty. They just stuffed her mouth with socks so she would keep quite while they raped her, and she suffocated. So tragic!

Chapter Six – Breaking a Curse

In August of 1986 I was working the night shift from 7:00 p.m. to 3:00 a.m. That night would prove to me several things that would become part of my career.

That evening after I went to work my wife, Stephanie, was home cleaning out a drawer. She found a poem. She had read this poem at high school speech meets. The poem was "Patterns" by Amy Lowell. The poem spoke of a young woman's lover soon to be her husband being killed in action. She had read this poem over and over at the speech meets. As she read the poem, she felt that there was danger on the job for me. She began to pray and break the "Patterns" of the poem of death of a lover as she had read over and over in school. She broke any curses of robbing us as a married couple. She also broke the spirit of death she felt strongly that night in the name of Jesus and by the power of His blood.

It may sound strange, but we can speak things over our lives without even knowing it. There is power in words.

When I got to work that night myself and Detective Steve Antuna were deciding what to do with the night. We were in the basement parking level of the police building getting ready to search a car on an unrelated homicide. We got a call from the Sergeant on the night shift Detective Bureau desk. The Sergeant told us that a suspect that I had a Homicide warrant for was at an apartment building in Aurora, which is a suburb east of Denver. The homicide case was only the second gang killing we had ever had up to that point. The suspect was a blood gang member named Darren Smith. Smith had shot and killed Herman Colbert on Herman's porch at 29th and Williams St. one hot summer evening.

Smith and two of his gang "homies" were walking down the street and got into a confrontation with Herman. Herman knocked Smiths hat off his head and the fight was on. Smith took out a .25 cal handgun and shot at Herman only to have Herman pull out his .357 Magnum and shoot back. Smith and his buddies ran off. Herman was confident that they would not return and stayed on his porch to enjoy his evening. The three snuck up on him with a sawed off shot gun and blew old Herman away. One of Herman's friends was shot in the leg.

We figured out who the shooter was after interviewing many gang members. We found out that none of them told the truth about anything. We finally put a case together and got a warrant for Smith. Smith was a blood gang member from California. In the meantime, Darrin had shot two other people. He was not proving to be a very up standing young man.

As we drove to the Aurora location the Detective Bureau desk Sergeant told us that a woman had called the Detective Division. The woman stated that Smith was in an apartment on the third floor with his shotgun. There was also a woman and some kids in the apartment. Smith was saying he would shoot it out with the police if they tried to come and get him. We notified the radio to call the Aurora police to meet us at the location and we took off. Detective Steve Antuna had been on the job a few years longer than me. He had been in Homicide for a few years. I had a great deal of respect for him as he was always impeccably dressed. He was very well spoken and very detailed. He was a good cop. I knew that from what I knew of his reputation not only in Homicide but knowing him when he worked the street. Many of the people you work with stay in your career for years either directly or indirectly. Sooner or later, you will cross each other's path again.

As we approached the building Aurora P.D. was still not there. The desk Sergeant was still in contact with the lady making the phone call. She was continually giving us information. We located the room on the third floor. I took up a position on the landing just below where I could look up and see the hallway. I would see the suspect if he entered or left the apartment. Steve went downstairs to wait for Aurora since we didn't have direct communication with them. I was watching the door with my gun, a nickel plated 6" Smith and Wesson .357 Magnum revolver, fitting to the legend. It was pointed up towards the landing with my right hand. My police radio in my left hand listening to the desk Sergeant. The Sergeant was telling me that the suspect was armed and would shoot it out.

A young black male child came out of the room. He started to walk towards me down the stairs. I stopped him and showed him a photograph of Darrin Smith. I asked if he was in the room and if he knew him. The little boy said "yes, that's my uncle Darrin". The child then walked down the stairs. I hoped Steve would detain him. Suddenly, a black male in his twenties came out of the room and looked directly at me. Our eyes met and I knew beyond a shadow of a doubt it was Darrin Smith. I could not see his hands completely. He turned to run back in the room. I was still hearing the sergeant on the police radio. He continued to tell me about the woman and children. He was also saying that Smith had a shotgun and would shoot it out with police. I don't even remember to this day pulling the trigger. All I remember is the smell of gunpowder and the sound that Smiths body made hitting the floor. It sounded like a sack of potatoes. I don't even remember hearing the shot. We were not allowed to use Magnum rounds. We used .38 caliber Police Hollow Points. There was a controversy before about the bullets we used when we had round nosed bullets.

That one hollow point did the trick that night. The Aurora PD just got there. Steve heard the gunshot. Steve told me later "I just knew you were OK, and it was the other guy". He never explained how he knew that, but I was glad he was right.

Just before anyone got there, I started up the stairs. I looked down past Smith lying on the floor. I saw this very heavy-set black lady holding a revolver that looked like Dirty Harry's 6" .44 Magnum. I started yelling at her to "drop the gun, drop the gun". I sure didn't want to shoot a lady. I think she was probably just trying to figure out what the heck was going on down the hall. She disappeared and I don't know to this day if the Aurora Detectives found her. I think she just heard the shot and wanted in on the action. Steve ran up the stairs and we approached the suspect with our guns pointed at him. He just kept saying "Why'd you do me?" I told him just don't die and prayed that he wouldn't.

After the ambulance and Aurora all arrived Steve and I drove to the Aurora Police Building.

While I was waiting for Aurora Detectives to get my statement several other people from the Denver Police Department showed up. The night shift Crimes against Person Sergeant showed up. He felt like he had to coach what I was going to tell the Aurora Detectives. My Captain from the Denver Police Crime against Persons Bureau showed up. He was a short red-haired guy we all called "Round and Red". He was nice enough and gave me his gun so I wouldn't feel unarmed. Aurora had to take my weapon from me for tests. Since this shooting took place in Aurora there wasn't much, he could do so he took off. The Denver Chief of Police showed up and asked if he could do anything for me. I asked if he could buy me a coke from the vending machine. I said, "yea that would be great". He didn't have enough change, so he also left. The Denver Deputy District Attorney on call also showed up then left since he couldn't be of help since the shooting was not in Denver. Good thing I knew Jesus cuss it was getting lonely.

I called home and told Stephanie what had happened and asked her to pray. She told me how she had found that poem. She had prayed for protection and provision over me right after she found it. God is an awesome God and gives us the desires of our hearts.

    My Attorney from the Police Protective Association, Dave Bruno showed up. I had known him for quite awhile and felt good about that. The Aurora Detectives said that they would have a nurse come and draw my blood to check for drugs and alcohol. My Attorney went crazy over their procedure. In Denver the procedure is different. We only take blood if there is a reason to believe the Officer Involved is under the influence. Then the Aurora Detective handling the case advised me of my rights. This also had the Attorney freaking out. In Denver we don't do that either. We give them a Garrity which is basically a promise to tell the truth, or they can be fired. My Attorney did not want me to make a statement at that time. He wanted me to make another time to come back. I knew how I would feel if I was handling a police shooting with one of our officers and he wanted to do that. I had to make a bold step and say that I had nothing to hide. I was going to give them a statement and tell them what happened against my Attorneys advice. The scripture says, "if God be for me who can be against me". Everything turned out good and it was called a "Justifiable Shooting" by the Adams County District Attorney. I later spoke to a friend of mine who works for another jurisdiction. He had talked to the Adams County District Attorney and was told that my level of cooperation helped them make their decision. They believed what I had said because I was cooperative with them and didn't play any games.

Smith went to trial and was convicted of 2nd Degree Murder for killing Herman Colbert. Darren Smith though would come back to haunt us again.

Chapter Seven – The Mission

    I want you to understand what makes a Homicide Detective tick at least from my perspective. Funny though as I write this book so much has changed in advances. Video cameras everywhere, new forensics. Just was different in those days. Our most effective tool was "KOD", knock on doors. I decided if I was going to work Homicide, I wanted to solve cases that no one had been able to solve yet. Maybe I could find something someone missed. Hopefully someone that was unknown would be found to be a witness. Many things can happen after a case has gone cold. There was a room in the basement of Police Headquarters that was called the "Homicide Room". That is where all the Homicides and Police Shootings were stored. When I first went down into the basement of Denver Police Headquarters to look at old homicide cases it struck me that in this room, that was about 25' by 15', there was a great deal of history of our city of Denver, all tragic. There are cases there dating back to the nineteen twenties that were one page long. "The suspects were found to have killed the victim. The police kicked in the door and arrested the suspect. The suspect went to court and was convicted." Police work sure seemed a lot easier back then, and it was. Then there were cases that had two or three folders full of information on a case. Some were in a real mess. I worked with some detectives that must have just wanted to call themselves "Homicide Detectives". They really didn't have the dedication or determination of some that really did want to do the job.

There was a real sense of death and sadness in the room. I asked older detectives that had worked in homicide in the past what cases they wanted to solve but didn't before they stopped working homicide. They always had at least one that still bugged them. Now I understand. I still, after being retired for many years and out of Homicide even longer think about cases. Unfortunately, I think of more than one. I think about them in the middle of the night and can't sleep.

Most people don't have a clue what it takes to solve a murder, only what they see on T.V. Just about everything you see on T.V. and the movies is phony. The good guys don't always win. They aren't always right but then again, they aren't wrong as much as the media tries to make you think. Cops are just people trying to do what they have been trained to do. The difference with homicide investigation is that to be good at it you must have a sixth sense or God, which works well for me!

As I looked for an old homicide to work on. I found one that really interested me. This case would be one of the greatest testimonies for God that I've seen. This was the case of the Gail Garcia-Herrera murder. There had been a lot of pressure from Gail's brother Gary Garcia to solve this case. Gail Garcia was a twenty-three-year-old woman. She married Phil Herrera not long after high school. Both were raised in North Denver. They went to North High School the same time Stephanie and I went there.

In the early years of marriage, they lived in the basement apartment of a home in North Denver. The two had some trouble in their marriage as a lot of young couple's encounter. They had a short time of separation. Rumor had it that Gail may have had a boyfriend named Chuck Wilson, a friend of her husband Phil. Rumors are one of the worst enemies to a homicide investigation. Especially an old one like this. The Herrera's had two small children a two-year-old boy named P.J. and a one-year-old girl, named Michelle. On April 27th, 1984, around noon a phone call came from the Herrera home at 4187 Winona Ct. from the Avon lady. P.J. answered the phone and told the Avon lady that mommy couldn't come to the phone and that he had put Kleenex in her "owies".

When the police arrived on that sunny April day they found Gail Garcia-Herrera stabbed to death on the bedroom floor. There was food on the floor of the home, apparently the kids had tried to take care of themselves. Only God knows what the children knew in their little spirits. Did they know their mommy was dead or did they just think she was sleeping?

In the original investigation a 911 tape was discovered that had an eerie conversation between a female and a 911 clerk. The call came in around midnight "Charlie don't, don't Charlie" over and over in a hysterical voice. Who was "Charlie"?

During the investigation information was developed that led to a school friend named "Charlie Wilson" everyone called Charlie Wilson "Chuck". No one called him Charlie. Charlie was a friend of the victim's husband, Phil Herrera. The rumors went around about Gail having an affair with Charlie, but all her closest friends said she despised Charlie Wilson. There were detectives that worked on the case, who suspected her own husband. A torment Phil would carry for years to come. For some reason no one had officially cleared Phil.

At least not that I could find any evidence of in the case. Phil was in Wyoming at work with the railroad. He was looking forward to coming home and going skiing with Gail that weekend only to arrive home from work to find the police at his home. He was not allowed to go into his home that he shared with his wife, son and daughter, which now is called "a crime scene".

Seeing this kind of tragedy affects the lives of many policemen. They harden their hearts in defense and develop a sick sense of humor to cover and overcome the feelings. I remember thinking about how I could have dealt with something like this and there just doesn't seem to be a way.

Phil claimed to have called Gail from Wyoming, but the call did not show up on the phone bill as a collect call. This was one of the things that allowed suspicion to point to Phil. This is the type of information that detectives will get hung up on and get tunnel vision because of it. At the same time, you cannot ignore it.

You must keep an open mind and not think killers would act the way you would act in any situation. One of the worst mistakes I saw in my career was when a detective would have in his mind how a person would act in any certain situation. There's just no way you can know these things and you can't use your experiences to prove a scenario. I saw Detectives try and put together a scenario using their own past, feelings and personalities. No can do unless you are a murderous pervert yourself. Yes, you can try and think that way. Of course, you can try but it is still best not to think you know what is in the killer's head. Don't get tunnel vision.

The detectives on the case in 1984 brought in Charlie Wilson for an interview. Wilson claimed that he had gone out to a party with a friend, Doug Wood. He then went to a bar in North Denver, The Berkley Inn, He said he was by himself, then went home to his wife Mary and slept the night. Wilson then called in sick from work the next morning. His wife, Mary, turned out to be a real problem in this case. A search warrant was run on Wilson's house. An illegal shotgun was found. Wilson was arrested for that charge as well as the murder of Gail. The Deputy District Attorney in charge of this case, Bill Ritter, decided to not go forward with the case against Charlie Wilson for the murder. A decision that bothered many at the time but turned out to be the best decision he could have made. If the case had gone to trial and Wilson had been acquitted Wilson would walk free for the murder. He could not have been tried again. Ritter felt that he could not prove beyond a reasonable doubt to a jury that the 911 tape was Gail. He did not know for sure that she was talking about Charles Wilson. He did not know if the tape would even be admissible in court. What if the case went to trial and because of the lack of evidence Wilson was acquitted? He would never have been able to be tried again according to the Constitutionality of Double Jeopardy. Ritter decided to drop the case and of course was criticized for it.

Bill Ritter became a friend of mine over the years. I think we had mutual respect. He left the District Attorney's Office for a time in 1987. He and his wife went on the mission field for the Catholic Church in Africa. After coming back to the D. A's office Ritter ran for District Attorney and was elected. He held the office until term limits forced him to quit in 2005. He then ran for Governor. By the way he was the first and last Democrat I ever voted for. He was elected. He played a key role in the filing of this case. His judgment to dismiss this case when it happened would prove to be right.

The years to come would be tormenting to Gail's family, especially to her brother Gary. Gary Garcia would eventually play a large part in keeping me motivated to see this case through.

When I first became a Homicide Detective in 1986, we had only eight Detectives, one Sergeant and a Lieutenant, who was also responsible for Sex Assaults, Robberies and Assaults.

When I first started our Lieutenant was Dave Michaud, who later went on to be Chief of police. Michaud was a great cop who liked to work hard and respected those that did the same. Our Sergeant at the time was John Thompson. He liked to try and intimidate you, but a sense of humor could diffuse it. When I got in the unit, I'm pretty sure it was Michaud that wanted me not Thompson so that was very awkward at times.

Of course, as time went on new cases would cause this one to go to the back burner. I wasn't the only detective that liked working on old cases. This was way before all the Cold Case Details started all over the country.

As with the Gail Garcia Herrera case time would go on, the case not forgotten. I continued to work on the case as time allowed between active cases for the next 12 years.

Chapter Eight – Murder Pinned on Wrong Man

In October of 1986 I was working the nightshift in Homicide and received a call on a Homicide at in the 1300 blk of Columbine St. When I arrived, I was told a female had been stabbed. She was taken to Denver General hospital where she was pronounced dead. Her name was Elodine Thornburg. There was a lot of blood on the sidewalk as well as a trash bag and a pair of pliers. There was also a pocketknife with blood on it on the ground. Det. Antuna was called from home. We began a search of the crime scene and talked to neighbors. Witnesses had heard the victim scream and a witness saw a black man run from the scene. Det. Antuna and I went into the victim's apartment. It was in the 1300 blk of Columbine St. We wanted to see if we could gain any information leading to a suspect. A weird thing happened. As we were looking through the victims' papers on her desk we found a church bulletin from Calvary Temple Church. Not only is that the church Stephanie and I went to, but our names were in the bulletin as cell group leaders. That felt strange. As the next day's went on, we received information that there was a witness that saw a black man in the bushes. As we continued the investigation, we found that there was a halfway house just a few blocks from the crime scene. We found that just minutes after the stabbing a person named Willis Brown had checked in to the halfway house. Sgt BJ Haze was the night shift Sergeant. He showed a line up to the witness that saw the black man run from the scene of the crime. The witness picked Willis Brown. After the case was shown on the news a bus driver called us with information. She said she remembers the Elodine being on her bus the night she was killed. She also identified the suspect being on her bus and getting off where the victim got off. Not looking good for Brown. We interviewed Brown's boss and asked if there had been any tools missing. His boss said that there was a pair of pliers that may be missing. This guy's goose is cooked.

We got an arrest warrant for him and arrested him. I spoke to him and advised him of his rights. He swore he had nothing to do with it. I saw what looked like a drop of blood on his shoes. We took those to test them. We walked him to the city jail and put him on the elevator. I felt a sick feeling in my stomach. I didn't think he was the guy. I was so convinced I went to the command at the time and told them so. This isn't the murderer. They looked at me and I thought "oops!" I'm in big trouble. I stayed adamant about it, but they said, "it's him".

The DA accepted the case and set it for preliminary hearing. About a month later I went to court. We had the preliminary hearing. After hearing all the evidence, the Judge held him over for trial. I turned to Deputy District Attorney Doug Wamsley and said, "I don't think he did it". Doug was feeling the same thing. I went home and tried to relax. I had started my vacation a few days earlier. The Preliminary Hearing was on the news that night.

Low and behold I got a phone call the next day. Two friends were watching the news. They were talking about the case. One guy turned to the other and said, "that guy didn't do it, I did".

The next day the paper read on the front page "Murder Pinned on wrong Man". I kept that newspaper headline on my desk for the rest of my career. I vowed that would never happen again.

Chapter Nine – Mr. Homicide

Joe Russell, who became one of my mentors, taught me how to pull a case apart and put it back together again. Joe had been kicked out of Homicide over a Homicide case that he and the command didn't see eye to eye on. Joe didn't back down to anyone. About 7 months after I started in Homicide and Sgt Haney now Lieutenant Haney came back to Homicide so followed Joe Russell. Finally, someone decided good for the department and not their ego. Joe was a quiet guy.

Joe was an older detective that was about 18 years my senior. He was the best. Joe was an Indian from South Dakota. He had kind of a flat head and used to say he jumped in an empty swimming pool when he was a kid. Those who loved him called him "Ingine Joe". He never gave up. But he also knew when there was no chance to solve one. Whether it was a new case or an old one, Joe just knew. He would also become a very close confidant. He always asked about the family and would give advice whether you wanted it or not. I lost my father right after I got on the job in 1976. I guess I looked for Joe's approval quite a bit.

Joe was tall and looked Indian. He loved to kid you but when he meant business you knew it was time to get serious. When he first came back into the Unit you could tell he didn't really like me. I was the youngest guy there at the time and had to win his approval. I had a homicide case at one of the Larimer Street Bars. Larimer Street was full of Mexican Bars and winos. He watched me as I went around talking to many people. I thought it was good information on the killer. The killer was a young Mexican male. He had used a .25 Caliber semi-automatic handgun. I thought I had a good suspect. I wanted to put him in a photo lineup. Joe got mad as we were driving around the area. Joe said that I was running around like a chicken with my head cut off. He informed me "this isn't the guy". Well, the witnesses identified the suspect in the photo lineup. To make matters better for me and worse for Joes opinion. The murder gun was found in a bush down the street. It not only matched the murder bullet but was registered to the suspect identified in the photo. Joe was cool to me after that.

I remember one time getting called out on a store owner who shot and killed a burglar in his place of business. It was around 4:00 a.m. I was the Primary Detective called out which meant it was my case. Joe was the secondary Detective on call and was also called out. The building was large and there was a ladder going to the roof. It was cold and snowing very hard that morning and I looked up the ladder and said, "hey Joe how about checking the roof for me". Joe looked a little surprised and said wait a minute I'm too old to go up there and it's snowing. I told him to go ahead and stop complaining. He would have told me to do if the shoe was on the other foot. When he came down, he was soaked and very cold. I don't think he ever forgave me for that morning.

Joe was great. As I said before He taught me how to pull an old case apart and start it all over. Joe let me work on an old case he opened of a man and woman that were shot in 1978. The suspect was known at that time, but they didn't have enough evidence to file a case. We re-interviewed all the witnesses and were able to not only file the case but get a conviction for two counts of First-Degree Murder.

The Homicide Unit was full of colorful characters at the time when we were the most effective. We had Lieutenant Tom Haney, who has been mentioned before, nice Irish boy. And yes, he had three brothers also on the job right out of a cop novel, right? He really was a homicide detective at heart. I had worked for him on the street when he was a sergeant, and as I said he made me interested in being in Homicide. He had the nickname of Father Haney. Everyone went to him with their problems.

We had two teams of 6 detectives with a Sergeant in charge of each team. Sergeant Dan Yount was the leader of the team I was on. Dan was the kind of guy that unless you wanted him to really fix something, don't tell him about it. Because before you knew it, he had jumped in it with both feet. I took a chance with Dan in that I told him how much I loved working Homicide. But made sure he understood my relationship with Christ and my family came first. Really never knew till years later how that went over but glad I spoke my mind. I had worked for him when he had been transferred in the Assault Unit right before I left. He seemed very by the book then. I wondered what it was going to be like working for him in Homicide.

Chapter Ten – Spiritual eyes

It wasn't long before I started to see the spiritual warfare that would mark my time in Homicide. I would start to identify things in certain types of homicides that would have very significant spiritual meaning. Of course, I could not talk with everyone about what I would see. Most other detectives already thought that I was strange because of my Christian beliefs. The devil is behind all the evil in the world, right? The word of God says that man's heart is deceitfully wicked. Does the devil give us all thoughts that we can reject or fulfill? How much does the devil influence day to day events? I would see God move in miraculous ways on murder cases that most would say were just coincidence but there was no way! I got interested in a case where a young mother was killed while her two children again a boy and a girl were at home when the killing occurred. The lady's husband found her dead in their bed raped and murdered. The small daughter was still swinging in her swing. This murder happened when I was still on the street in 1978. I remember going door to door at that time trying to help the detectives solve the case. The main theory was that a young boy who lived across the street had killed the woman. The small boy told detectives that it was a tall black person that looked like a basketball player. This led them to believe the person was wearing some kind of sports team jersey. There was a note pad lying next to the front door. There was also a bottle of spermicidal foam in the bedroom. This may lead the investigators to believe that the suspect knew that would ruin any evidence. Any evidence at the scene in the way of sperm would be destroyed. This case would bother me my entire career and to this day. In about 1990 I had the Crime Lab go over all the evidence again. They found semen that they had not found before on the bed spread. At this time with the DNA testing that could be done we could possibly have evidence to use if we found a suspect. One of my superiors thought I wasted my time working on old cases. He just didn't have the homicide detective's mentality. I began to eliminate the suspects that we had starting with the husband. That was very difficult to contact him and even bring up the case. I drove by the house one afternoon where the murder happened. I realized that he and his two children as well as his new wife still lived in the house. I noticed a young girl that was in the yard and a chill went down my spine as I thought it was the victim in real life. It was the daughter. Sometimes the photos of a murder scene are imprinted in your mind forever. The children were too young when this occurred to benefit from talking with them, so I just tried to eliminate the suspects. The husband was very cooperative. I eliminated him right away by comparing his DNA to the crime scene. I was able to find the young man that everyone thought did it. He was eliminated through DNA testing. There was one more long shot that I started to believe could be the real answer to this mystery. As I said before, in 1978 I was on a team that assisted in this case. I remember that we checked out a car that had apparently broken down across the street from the victim's home. That fits with my theory that someone came to the door asking to use the phone. Maybe Madeline let him write down a number on the pad or she wrote down a number for him. Then he forced his way into her home. The man fit the description of being black. He was checked out somewhat when the incident occurred. He didn't really have a good alibi. I started to put together a 41.1 which is what I needed for the young man and the husband for their blood. It is a search warrant for what is referred to as nontestimonial evidence. This is evidence taken from a suspect's body such as blood, hair or fingerprints. I finally found the person and served him with the warrant. I took him to the crime lab and his blood was taken. Unfortunately, it didn't match the evidence from the crime scene. But at least another suspect was eliminated.

This is one of those cases that you never forget. When time permits you come back to and try again until there is just nowhere to go. If people knew how much I depended on God, they would understand. They would know why awesome things happened during the cases. Some just thought I had a knack for knowing if someone was telling the truth. It was God showing me or my wife and me. Many times, I would look into the eyes of a killer and see the demon that manipulated them. Or the hollow look in their eyes showing no emotion would try and intimidate me.

After I retired, I would still think of this case, sometimes in the middle of the night. It was a case I always regretted not solving before I left Homicide. Strange twist that happened in 2023. Through DNA a suspect was developed. Turns out the suspect had been in jail for killing an Aurora Policewoman not long after the homicide. His DNA pointed to a total of 5 woman that he killed. The suspect had died in jail. I never think about it in the middle of the night any longer. Justice was served and the innocent blood was avenged.

Going back to the case of Gail Garcia Herrera. As time passed, I continued to get small pieces of information but could not get Bill

Ritter, who was now the District Attorney of Denver, to file the case against Charlie Wilson. I told Ritter I wasn't going to give up. We received information that Charlie was in prison in Minnesota and had been moved there from Taos New Mexico. He was convicted of two sexual assaults there. One he forced his way into victim's apartment and one he knew the victim. Both cases were like what we believed happened in our case. I connected with the detective in Taos and verified all the information. I found one of the witnesses that was with Charlie on the night of the murder. I verified that that night he had a large knife the night of the murder. The witness stated he was afraid to tell the police about it that night. The main force in getting this case filed in court was not only good police work but constant prayer. Stephanie and I prayed about this case all the time. We continued to pray for a breakthrough. We got very specific and prayed that somehow Charlie would confess to someone in jail and more witnesses would come forward. We also knew the Garcia family was praying and would never give up hope. Det. Hemphill and I found Charlie's wife, Mary, who had moved back to Denver. She stuck to her original story that Charlie was home the night of the murder. She also knew now that we were not going to give up and this was not going away! At the time of the homicide the coroner found sperm in the victim's body. There wasn't much they could do with that in 1984. And at best it would only prove Gail had sex with someone or even Charlie.

Chapter Eleven – Not him again

Remember I said that the guy I shot came back? Well, here is the readers digest version of the story. There had been a robbery where a guy was arrested. The suspect knew there was witnesses to his crime and set out to have them killed from jail. We always told people "Don't worry we will protect you". I never said that again. So, this suspect used his girlfriend to set up two of his henchmen to go to the witness's house and shoot them. So, one night very late they waited for two of the witnesses to show up and shot both in the backyard of their home. There was a third person not involved in the robbery as a witness that was in the house. This person was put down on the ground face first. One of the shooters stood over him and prepared to shoot him in the back of the head. He fired his gun, and the victim started to bleed and did not move. The suspect fled the house. That victim was alive! He was brought to the Homicide Unit, and I interviewed him. Turned out I knew his Father because we all went to the same church. This victim told me that as he lay there knowing he was going to be shot, he "prayed in tongues" under his breath. He was able to lay still even though he was grazed by a bullet, and it saved his life. The suspect thought he was dead because of the amount of blood.

    Lieutenant Haney and I arrested the girlfriend. She was about 350 lbs. As the investigation continued the parties were identified. The plot reveled the guy in jail for robbery decided to hire someone to kill another witness. Now he would be responsible for two killings.

Then a third, his girlfriend, if completed. He had figured she must have told the police everything. The girlfriend was shot several times with a .25 Caliber pistol but lived. Hemphill and I went to the hospital and talked to the girlfriend. She identified the shooter as none other than Darren Smith. The guy I shot in 1986. Smiths' conviction for killing Herman was overturned. It was overturned on the grounds that his accomplices testified against him. Back to prison for Smith.

The Girlfriend told us that the doctor told her that none of the bullets passed through her fat and that "your too fat to die".

Chapter Twelve – Ready set Go!

Working Homicide as I have said was a never-ending roller coaster. You just never knew what to expect next, or when. One day two Detectives from Weld County came to Denver and asked us to help them in a case. The decomposed body of a woman by the name of Fran De-Perez was found along the side of a road in rural Colorado. Her body had been there for almost a month. Perez was found to be from Denver. The detectives had found out that she was last seen with her boyfriend who also lived in Denver. The man's name was Dennis Magana. Sergeant Doug Hilderbrant and I offered to help in the case. Doug was a balding well-built very well-dressed man. He had a way of letting you know when he meant business. We used to joke that if you could look into his eyes and could see the back of his head you knew it was time to get serious. He was an experienced investigator that liked to get involved in cases. It wasn't too hard to find this fella Magana as the Weld County detectives knew where he worked. We all went out and picked him up. We asked him if he would please come to HQ so we could talk with him, and he consented. Since no one had probable cause to get an arrest warrant for him he could have said "no". When we got to HQ Doug and the Weld County detectives spoke with Magana for about an hour with no results. I asked if I could give it a try and they said "sure". I then spent about four hours with Magana. I found out that we went to high school at the same school at the same time. We knew a lot of the same people. I would throw out scripture about how the innocent blood cries out from the grave for justice. This story is in the bible when Cain killed his brother Abel. We would talk about people we knew and what may have happened to them now. We also talked about Magana being a Christian in school. Magana was getting very close to confessing to killing Perez when he said, "I'll tell you about it, but I want a lawyer". Well that usually means the interview is over. If someone says they want a lawyer, you must stop the interview which I did. I walked out of the room with the other detectives looking at me with disappointment. I called my wife Stephanie and told her the story. Stephanie asked me if I prayed. I said, "well sort of, I gave the guy a lot of scripture". I explained to Stephanie that if someone asks for a lawyer you can't talk to him anymore unless the person initiates the conversation. So that's how she prayed! She also prayed that the innocent blood would be avenged. Stephanie prayed that he would come out of the room and ask to talk with me. I got done talking with Stephanie and hung up the phone. I went over to my desk to talk with the detectives. About 10 minutes went by as we were discussing what to do next. Magana came out of the room and said "Joe, I want to tell you about it now!". I went back in the room and Magana told me about how he had stabbed Perez in the kitchen in his apartment. He then rolled her body up in a carpet and put it in the trunk of his car. He went to work the next day and took her to where he dumped her body. We put Magana in jail and obtained a search warrant to go to his apartment and collect any evidence. The apartment house was only 4 blocks from the house that I lived in as child. We went to the apartment after dark so we could use a technique known as Luminal. Luminal is a chemical that when sprayed on an area where there had been blood it shows in the dark. Even if it had been cleaned up the blood will show a florescent color shining in the dark. Thus, the scripture again proves to be true "the innocent blood cries from the grave". The crime lab did not have an actual camera to photograph the results of the test. The crime lab sergeant, Sgt Paul Selander, did a great job of going to the sporting goods store and buying a clamp.

Now he could clamp an infrared night scope to the lens of a video camera, and it worked great. When all the lights were turned out and the lab detective started to spray the chemical the results caused many remarks from the detectives on the scene. Everyone was in such amazement the audio had to be turned off on the video camera so as not to record the remarks we all made. The blood was crying out just like the bible says. It was an amazing image of Gods word coming to life. This was the first time the Denver Police Department used luminol. Since the murder happened in Denver we took the case.

The Lord showed us that this was another example of the scripture in Genesis 4:10 "Your brother's blood cries out to me from the ground".

This scripture as we said is the basis of this book. God moves in anyone's life that prays and ask for Him to intervene. The cases in this book are not the only time we have seen God move in my experience in police work. Miracles do happen. So many things have happened in my 33 years in law enforcement to prove Gods love and intervention.

Of course, this is just the beginning of convicting a killer. First, we do all the crime scene work and interview all the witnesses. We then spend hours typing everything up to make sense and try not to forget anything. We may not think something is important, but it needs to be documented. We must convince the District Attorney's Office that we have a good case. Sometimes that was a lot of fun. Sometimes it made you mad as hell because they didn't want the case. The complaint Deputy in this case had no problem taking this case with the evidence we had. In this case the District Attorney that was assigned the case for trial had a problem with the biblical sound of the interview. Now what is that all about? There was nothing done improper in that interview. Oh, did I mention this was the second girl this guy stabbed? The first one lived. Anyway, the District Attorney decided to give Magana a plea bargain and let him plead guilty to Second Degree Murder. What a joke. I have no problem with some plea bargains but not when there was nothing wrong with the case. Well Magana may or may not still be in prison, but God is the ultimate judge. I always tried to make sure I did everything by the book so as not to lose any evidence or interview in court. I was soon to find out that I did not always have control over those things no matter how hard I tried.

Chapter Thirteen – Still small voice

Sometimes a Detective wanted to be in Homicide just to say they were a Homicide Detective, I guess. There were a few in the time I worked there that I sure could never figure out why they were there. Take home car? Paid overtime? I worked with one guy that every time the "Bat Line", we called it, rang you could rest assured he would look up from his desk look both ways and leave the room. That way if it was a Homicide he wouldn't have to go and maybe the Sergeant would not notice he was gone. I'll call him Detective Caputo. Anyway, one afternoon we got a call to the Capitol Hill area of Denver named after the State Capitol being in the neighborhood. Same area I worked when I was in patrol.

    This area at the time was full of con artists, drug dealers and prostitutes. It had the highest crime rate in the city. Caputo got stuck and had to go. For this one I wish he had gotten out of the office in time. The Homicide was on the second floor of an apartment building on Pearl St. just one block down from the famous Colfax Ave. Colfax is said to be the longest business street in the world. As I said before I worked this area when I was a Patrolman, it was an evil place to work no doubt about it. Det. Calvin Hemphill and I entered the room and saw a very modest room with a couple of chairs and a bed. There was a sink and a small stove and that was about it. There was a male body laying on the bed with a large hole in his head. Calvin and I thought he had been hit with something. The Lieutenant from the crime lab showed up and promptly informed us that the man had been shot in the head. There was what looked like a bloody bugger on the wall going down the stairs from the second floor. The on-call Deputy DA showed up long enough to come in and stumble on a small box on the floor. We invited them all to leave so we could process the crime scene. Now Hemphill was a top-notch Detective, very opinionated but top notch and usually too outspoken for his own good. We worked a lot of cases together. Calvin went around the apartment building talking to folks. He came back and said that he had talked with the manager. The manager said he had seen a black man with the victim several days ago. The man was wearing radio headphones. Wham, I knew who it was. I believe God allowed me to remember his name immediately and I said it's Norris Jones, he's the guy. I used to see him on Colfax Ave. when I worked on the street which would have been at least 7 years before. Calvin looked at me like I was nuts and Caputo just smiled because he knew I was nuts. Calvin took off and we finished up the crime scene. The Coroners Office took the body to the morgue after the coroner verified that the victim had been hit in the head with something.

    I looked at Caputo and said let's go look for Jones. He said you "gotta be kiddin?" No let's just look I'll bet he is right there on the corner at Colfax and Pearl St in the White Spot Restaurant. We pulled into the parking lot and went inside. There were several booths on the left and a long counter on our right. As we got to the end of the counter there, Norris was sitting at the counter wearing several coats and of course his headphones. He remembered me right away and said hi "Cigar" that was my nick name as I had said before. It stuck with a lot of folks even when I was retired and hadn't smoked in over 38 years. We patted old Norris down, but he had so many layers of clothes on it was impossible to do a good job. We asked him if he would come to Police HQ with us and that we were going to handcuff him because we could not pat him down properly. Norris said that he would. We drove to the crime scene and the manager said that was the person he saw with the victim. We then went to HQ. As I took Norris to the Sergeants office to talk with him Det. Caputo went to the ID Bureau to get Jones' record and see if he had any outstanding warrants and found one.

I advised Norris of his Miranda rights which he waived. We sat and talked for a long time. Norris denied having anything to do with killing the victim. After listening to him for awhile I decided to bluff him. I told him that his fingerprint was in that bloody bugger going down the wall. He bought it. Now the story was that the victim tried to rape him, and he had to fight him off by hitting him with a hammer. He said he threw the hammer on the roof. Guess the Crime Lab Lieutenant was wrong, as if we didn't know.

After the confession we went back to the scene and found the ball peen hammer on the roof of the apartment building. The case seemed open and shut. So on to the suppression hearing. That's where the defense tries to suppress any evidence that the Prosecution has and tries to keep it from the jury.

The case was assigned a Public Defender, Mary Smith, who was on many of my cases. She caught me in the hall at court during this case and asked me why people talk to me and tell me everything. I told her they just liked me, I guess. Then I asked her how she gets on so many of my cases "is it the classic case of good against evil?" She said, "something like that".

Several problems came up in this case. Mary Smith argued that there had to be something wrong with this case and Det. DeMott because this is the fastest solved case in the history of Colorado. She went on to argue that we did not have probable cause to arrest Jones in the first place. That all came about during Det. Caputo's testimony. Caputo testified that he did not hear the entire conversation between me and Jones and did not know why I handcuffed him. Caputo said, "well Det. DeMott mumbles you know". Thus, handcuffing was deemed an arrest. Then Caputo could not remember when he had found the warrant on Jones in conjunction with the interview I was having with Jones. One of the court employees during a break asked me if Det. Caputo was on our side. So, the Judge said Jones was being held against his will without probable cause. I believe in the law. I know that there must be protection and that everyone deserves a fair trial. But this was not going to turn out fair for the victim. So, Judge Markson, who I had testified in front of many times, found that the confession could not be shown to the jury. That made recovery of the murder weapon "the fruit of the poisonous tree". So that could not be shown to the jury. Jones was advised of his rights and did not have to talk but instead he did and ended up confessing but would be set free. There was no way we could convict Jones with what we had left to show the jury. Then boom God made His move. I will never understand what happened next except it had to be God because Smith would not have allowed this under her own power. She cared nothing for these victims, only her record. She let Jones pled guilty to Manslaughter. We win she loses, and Jones gets the max of 18 months in jail.

    Now here is the real clincher. About three years later I am at Lakeside Amusement Park with my family. Who do I see running one of the rides? You got it, Norris Jones. Our eyes met and I smiled, and he looked at me sheepishly and said, "Hi Cigar". I started to talk to him about the Lord and he said that he had accepted Jesus in jail. I gave him a big hug and said that's great.

Chapter Fourteen - Do something, something happens

I was trying to remember cases where the Lord had His hand in the suspects getting caught. I asked some retired guys I had worked with to help me remember some cases that would fit this scenario. Calvin Hemphill brought up one that I did not think of for this book until I heard Calvin say "Slim, God must have wanted that guy caught".

Bill Allen lived in Park Hill in a small white house on the corner. He was found stabbed to death one afternoon by his wife. The victim had been stabbed numerous times and there seemed to be no real motive. Robbery must have been the motive. Det. Dave Pontarelli was called out on the case. Dave was a great guy and worked hard on his cases. Park Hill is a neighborhood where there are very expensive homes to the south and not so expensive to the north. There is a lot of gang activity as well as drugs and burglaries. There was no evidence at the scene leading to a suspect.

A few days after the murder I asked Calvin to go with me to just go look around the neighborhood and talk to people. We went into a bar in the neighborhood and just asked around to see if anyone had heard anything about the murder. No one had. My attention was drawn to a tall skinny black male around 35 years old. He said his name was Robert Woods, he said they call me "Slim". He said he didn't know about the murder.

About a week or so after the murder we got a call from a lady who said she had heard that some tall skinny black male called "Slim" had killed Bill. What a deal! Short chapter for this case. Pontarelli came to my retirement ceremony and made a big deal about this case telling the crowd how it amazed him how I solved this case. He also said that my drawings of victims looked like "Gumby". Most cops would say it was just a good old "KOD" Knock on Doors. Really it was "GOD"!

Chapter Fifteen – The Abyss

Most people never really see how evil the world is. People are very cruel and heartless. Of course, many are desensitized on what they see on TV and in the Movies. There was a quote on the wall in the Homicide Unit for awhile. I never knew where it came from, but it was:

"When you stare into the abyss the abyss stares back at you." — Friedrich Nietzsche.

Well, I had the opportunity to do just that in this case.

There was a Barber on East Colfax Ave that was well known and very loved by the folks in the city. He was known as "Barber Bob" his name was Robert "Bobbie" Willis. One sunny afternoon Barber Bob cut the hair of a not so nice customer. The man complained that Barber Bob messed up his hair and was very angry. An argument ensued and went out into the street. The Police were called, and Officer Dave Lusk responded and told the angry man to leave which he finally did. Not very long after the Officer left the angry man came back and shot Barber Bob dead. The neighborhood was in shock and very angry. Some blamed the officer for not doing anything when he was there on the disturbance call. What could he have done?

It didn't take too long before we identified the killer as a Paul Williams. An arrest warrant was issued for 1st Degree Murder. The hunt was on. We searched everywhere Williams was associated with. We did our best to find him. Finally, information was received that he was held up in an apartment on the west side of town.

It was around 10:00 pm when several of us converged on the parking lot of the apartment building. Dan Yount was our Sergeant. Dan was a very interesting guy. I had told him about Jesus many times. He would listen but really wasn't interested. One time we were working on a case where a guy had shot two people. We were on a stake out in a Home Depot parking lot drinking terrible 7-11 coffee. I just kept telling him about Jesus whether he liked it or not. You never know what seeds you plant will grow. He was very by the book. Anyway, I liked him. I remember we were dog tired, as we were in so many of these cases. You worked until there was no more steam and sometimes you kept working. We tried to put together a plan to arrest Williams. We checked out the apartments and there were only a few apartments in a rundown one-story building. The room Williams was reported to be in was at the end of a long dark hallway. It was decided that Yount and I would go first and sneak down the hallway in the dark. I carried a bullet proof vest in my trunk and slipped it on, Yount followed me. It was a little hairy sneaking down the hallway. We had the key to the apartment. As we approached the door Yount put the key in the lock and quickly turned it as we pushed open the door yelling Police!!! I will never forget seeing Williams laying in the bed as I stuck my Smith and Wesson 9mm in his eye so hard that the slide on the weapon started to go back.

As I looked at him, he at me he smiled. Yes, I was looking in the Abyss and it was looking back at me.

When we went to court the jury was obviously shaken by the suspects smile. He was convicted.

There had been several incidents that occurred that really brought us to understand how we had to pray and protect ourselves and our family. We had a case where a man and woman had been shot and the house set on fire. That night I came home from the homicide we had a sunlamp catch a blanket on fire in our solar room. Coincidence? From that time, we prayed to protect us against the spirit of death. We also prayed for the cleansing of any demonic spirits following me home.

As the years went by, Dan Yount worked several more assignments and was promoted to Lieutenant. I saw him one day and started immediately telling him about Jesus. He told me it was too late he had accepted the Lord. I was so happy.

Chapter Sixteen – Lonely days, lonely nights

You never knew what the day or night would hold. Many days went by with no Homicides. That's when I had the time to work on the old ones. Of course, the days were also full of hours in court and studying for court. Somedays everyone was in the office. Other days detectives were off or on vacation or stuck in court for days or weeks. When you heard the radio crackle and the dispatcher say, "any Homicide Detective". Your adrenalin would kick in and you would answer the radio. The dispatcher would give you the info you needed to know, Homicide, Shooting, Stabbing, Suicide or a DOA. The dispatcher would give the address and who else might be responding such as the Crime Lab, Medical Examiner etc.... Sometimes you were the only one that answered the radio. Many times, you got to the scene not knowing what you had to deal with. You must assess the situation and decide if you need more help. If you are going to need a search warrant, the DA, a supervisor or maybe the PIO (Police Information Officer). The PIO helps with the press if they are on the scene.

Sometimes it's just you and another detective. Or maybe the Supervisor was in the office when the call came in and saw he had a room full of detectives and said, "let's go".

This case was one of those. We arrived to find a large three-story brick apartment building in the southwest part of town.

There was a dead girl that appeared to be raped. Sergeant Hilderbrant and several of us went to the scene. The partially nude body of a woman in her 30's was in the utility room. The utility room was on the third floor of an apartment building with about 7 rooms on each floor. The woman appeared to have been strangled to death and sexually assaulted. She was identified as Diane Van Norman, a resident of the building. Several detectives and patrolman went door to door to try and find a witness to the murder. Of course, hoping to talk to the killer himself and notice something suspicious in his demeanor or his story. Notes were left on the doors that no one answered asking them to contact the Homicide Unit as soon as possible. Unfortunately, no witnesses or suspicious men were located. Friends and relatives of the victim also could be of no help with any useful information.

Just like in many cases before, we did what we could as the day became night. We compiled all the information we had, which was basically nothing. Time to go home and get some sleep tomorrow would likely be a busy day.

As the next day started, we all talked about the endless possibilities of this case. Who was the last person that was with the victim, who did she hang around with? Boyfriends, girlfriends etc... A murder victim usually loses all privacy and sometimes any dignity by the time we were done digging into their past and present. We were ready to really start getting after anyone that may have known something when lunch time rolled around. Everyone decided to take off and get something to eat before the endless day really got going. There were just two stragglers, me and Det. Calvin Hemphill. Just as we were getting ready to leave the office the desk detective called. He said there was someone from the victim's apartment house at the desk that had gotten the message we had left to contact us. He thought he would just come on down.

A little upset that now we couldn't go to lunch Calvin, and I started the interview. The man that came to the office was Benton Scott. He lived in the apartment building that the victim lived in. He was a white male in his twenties. He was wearing a white "t" shirt and shorts. He had minor redness on his knees. He seemed to be wanting just to be helpful and respond to our request of all the apartment residences. As the interview went on both Calvin, and I started to get a little more aggressive in our questioning. Without talking to one another we both started to feel that this guy may be the killer. We stepped outside and decided we needed to advise this guy of his rights and go for it.

We pointed to several notebooks that held Homicide cases that were in the office. I pointed to them and said "you know we will be able to prove who did this by matching the semen of the suspect to the semen found in the victim's body from the rape. Back in that time we did not have DNA yet, but we could come very close with what forensic science we did have. So maybe I fudged a little. Then I started to go after the slight redness on his knees telling him that he was obviously the guy we were looking for. I pulled one of the cases off the shelf and pointed out some of the blood work reports. This would show him how it would look when our information came back. Showing us, he was the guy.

Didn't take long for him to roll! He was our guy. He told us the whole sordid story of how he raped this poor woman in the laundry room of their apartment house. How he strangled her last breath out of her with his bare hands.

After we got the story from him, we took him into the video room and both Calvin and I got the whole story on video.

We allowed him to smoke as he told his story. I will never forget how he explained how he strangled this woman. Calvin asked him "how did you choke her". Scott put his cigarette in his mouth and held it tight with his pierced lips. He held up his hands in the formation of choking someone and said, "the usual way". Even as I am writing this again so many years later, I feel the same chill we had then.

And I realized again what this meant:

"When you stare into the abyss the abyss stares back at you." — Friedrich Nietzsche

My wife experienced the abyss. One night Stephanie and I were out when I was on call. I got a call that a woman had been found dead and they did not know if she had been murdered. I was told to respond to HQ where I met the night shift Sergeant. He was interviewing a man that may had been involved with the woman. I was operating the camera in the video room and Stephanie was in the room with me. There was a one-way window in the room. We could see the subjects, but they could not see us. I left the camera and Stephanie alone. Suddenly the man looked right at Stephanie as if he could see her. He had a very evil look in his eyes as if to say, "I'm coming after you". That night she could see the "Abyss". The spirit on that guy knew the spirit of God on Stephanie and reacted! It was so real that Stephanie said" I thought you said he couldn't see me?" Turns out the lady died of natural causes. The evil was still there.

Before the trail of Benton Scott, Deputy D.A. Dave Conners called Calvin and I into his office. Conners was the Deputy D.A. assigned that would be prosecuting Scott in court. Conners had kind of an exaggerated way of speaking. It kind of reminded me of James Cagney. He was very upset as we told him how the interview with Scott unfolded. Conners told me that I was wrong in lying to Scott that we could make a positive identification from the semen sample and his blood. Well, the fight was on. I told him as far as I knew the law stated that you can tell a suspect anything you want if you don't go as far as telling him something that would make an innocent man confess. He went on and on and so did we.

On May 9, 1988, Benton Scott was found guilty of First-Degree Murder. Deputy D.A. Dave Conners wrote Calvin and I a nice letter of commendation. The letter read "the detective interrogation was among the best I have ever seen produced by any police officer". Well, guess he changed his mind. Anyway, God was there as usual to see that justice was done, despite all of us.

Chapter Seventeen– Dreams and Visions

One of the toughest things about working homicide is the unknown. The interference in your family life can be unbearable. You never know if you're going to make date night with your wife, or birthdays and holidays with your kid. We switched off every other week as to what team was on call from 3:30 pm till the next day. If a call came in while we were still there anything goes. Det. Tony Widmayer was another great detective. Great sense of humor and dedication. Kind of looked like a movie star.

We received a call that there had been a robbery at a southwest Denver liquor store. The owner of the store was a woman, and she had been stabbed numerous times. Tony and I as well as Sgt. Yount responded to the scene. It was a violent scene. There were tuffs of female hair all over the place as well as blood everywhere. Obviously, the owner put up a fight. These kinds of scenes usually mean the suspect knew the victim. The owner died of her wounds. There was no evidence at the scene to link to a suspect. Again, these were the days before you could just give a computer a DNA sample and boom you get a suspect. One witness that thought they saw someone leaving the store said that the man had a tattoo of a knife on his arm. That little piece of info cost many man hours to try and track down. Eventually the case got cold.

Throughout my police career my wife Stephanie was very helpful as I said before. We would pray about the cases. Stephanie would have dreams about situations or locations. Sometimes we were not able to figure out if they were connected to a case or which case. She had a dream one time about a woman being shot right near a phone booth where there were glass windows everywhere. Eventually that fit into a case where a prostitute was gunned down in exactly the type of area she dreamed of. Unfortunately, we never were able to use the info, but it made us more aware, and we prayed more. It was hard on Stephanie at times. Having these dreams that were very real and not knowing for sure what they meant.

Our son Joseph was a teenager at the time, and someone had broken into his car and stole his stereo. We prayed that whoever took it would be convicted and would return it. Yes, that happened. A kid that went to the same school took it and returned it. So that's right, we just prayed.

During this same time frame of the woman being killed in the liquor store Stephanie had a dream. The dream was about a guy cleaning rugs then killing a woman victim. There was no murder that had a carpet connection that we knew of at the time. We prayed that God would reveal what the dream was about, and the person would turn themselves in.

One day Det. Widmayer got a call from the Grand Junction Police Department which is about 5 hours from Denver. Some guy walked into their station and confessed to killing the liquor store owner.

Oh yes, he did know the victim, he had cleaned her rugs. Prayer does work. God does speak to His people. Listening is the key, knowing His voice.

When I told Det Widmayer about the dream he just said, "I believe it".

Chapter Eighteen – No way

As many of you know that watch crime dramas or re-enactments of murders on television know there is a medical process in every case. Forensic pathology is a science. You watch shows that have all these Coroners and Medical examiners and how they have helped solve murder cases. Some that have been hindered by false opinions and human error. One of the most grievous cases that I worked on was very tragic. At the time I was working with a female detective that I will name Det. Jones. She spent years in child abuse cases and was very good at her specialty. The only drawback to working with this person was she carried her gun in her purse. It seemed a little unsafe to me. Anyway, we got a call on a dead 6-month-old baby boy that was being cared for by a babysitter in the basement of the babysitter's home.

When we arrived, the scene looked like a normal clean home where small children and babies were being cared for. The babysitter was a white female in her twenties. She was very distraught that this baby had died in her care. She said that she had put the baby down for a nap and when she checked on the baby, she noticed that he was not breathing and was limp, she called 911. The baby had been in the same position as the babysitter left him.

Of course, we handled the case as a suspicious death from the beginning. The baby was transported to the hospital and pronounced dead then taken to the Denver Coroner's Office. I will refer to the coroner in this case as Dr. Smith. Of course, I had worked with this doctor on many occasions. I had known him to be thorough and competent. Not this time.

Dr. Smith concluded that the baby had injuries to his skull consistent with being picked up by the legs and smashed into a concrete wall. Those are some very serious injuries. How does that happen when all you have done is put a baby down for a nap?

Obviously and rightfully so our attention was focused on the babysitter. She had stated that there was no one else in the house with her except other children she was watching. Sergeant Hildebrant was deeply involved in this case. We as cops can say and try and act like these cases don't bother us. Most will say that cases involving children will always affect even the most seasoned veteran. And in this case that was true for all of us.

I had a gut feeling something was not right. I didn't feel this babysitter was involved. Being a Christian many Detectives thought sometimes I was soft. Maybe I gave too many too much benefit of the doubt. But that was not it. This is one of those times that I really feel God was speaking in that "still small voice". It wasn't because I was a hot shot great detective. The next step would be to give the babysitter a polygraph test. She did not pass it totally or as they say it was "inconclusive". Hildebrant and Det. Jones were really interrogating the babysitter. Really coming in for the kill. I stood my ground and told them she did not kill this baby. Of course, they thought I was nuts, which I can understand. The babysitter was not under arrest. She was asked to come to the Homicide Unit again. The plan was that Hildebrant and Jones were really going to go after her and hope for a confession.

The babysitter agreed to come in but would have to bring in one of the children she was still watching. A little 6-year-old boy that was at the house when the baby was napping. I took on the job as babysitter to the little boy. At that time there was a table in the hallway as you entered the Crime Against Persons Bureau that had books on it. Some were children's books. He was very quiet and well behaved. There was one book that had a ball and an elephant on the front. I took it and the little boy in one of the offices. I let the little boy look at the book. He started saying things like "that's what happened". The picture he was looking at was a bear falling off the ball and hitting his head on the ground. I just let him talk and tried not to lead him in anyway. I finally asked him if he saw what happened to the little baby at the house. He said he knew what happened. I asked him to tell me. He said that he picked up the baby when he was sleeping and held him up to his chest. He said the baby tried to bite him on the chest and he threw the baby backwards and the baby hit his head on a the side of a table. He said he "picked the baby up and put him back in his bed and covered him up again".

I immediately called one of the Deputy District Attorneys that handled Child Abuse cases. This DA had a reputation of being a real jerk sometimes and I was a little concerned. She arrived and again together we listened to the little boy repeat his story. We were convinced this was what really happened. The babysitter was not charged. Again, God came through. Not for me but for justice, God loves justice.

Going back to the Gail Garcia Herrera case. We finally had enough evidence to get a 41.1 for Charlie's blood and hair so we could see if the sperm matched. Now we had DNA. I wrote up the 41.1 which basically is nontestimonial evidence and like a search warrant. The DA must approve it before the Judge signs approves and signs it. The situation here remember is Charlie is in Prison in Minnesota, so I had to have a detective from there serve the warrant and collect the evidence, they did so joyfully! Now we wait for several months in those days.

After months we received word, we had a one in 11 million people match. On top of that our prayers about people coming forward also paid off. I begged DA Ritter to file the case. No way was I giving up now it had to be done!!! He agreed and the suspect was transported to Denver and placed first in the city jail then to the county jail.

When Charlie was in the county he had a cell mate. He told the cell mate that he killed Gail. The info was not needed in court and not brought up but thank you Jesus!!! We had it if we needed it! DA Bill Ritter finally accepted the case. Now the wait for trial.

Final Chapter Nineteen – The beginning of the end

In late 1996 we had had a lot of changes in command of the Homicide Unit and things began to change. We have a new Sergeant on my team and a new Division Chief of Investigations. Things just were not the same. You could feel the tension every time there was a homicide. The Lieutenant was acting very strangely and although I had thought respected me now started to ridicule me. This was the Lieutenant that always asked me "why do you work on these old cases?". In November of 1996 the whole unit was called out on a gang homicide in the 4300 block of Newton St. The suspect had shot the victim, Ray Garcia, many times with a rifle. Then he finished him off with a shotgun blast to the face. The entire unit except me had been called out. I never understood what that was all about. But when the radio room finally did call me late into the investigation and told me to respond to HQ, the Captain was furious. Someone there told him that I was ordered there.

I jumped in and tried to help. There were witnesses and Hispanic Gang Bangers all over the third floor. Up and down the halls, in all the interview rooms. As the evening became the next day there was no one left. All the witnesses were gone as well as the detectives. There were one or two detectives left, Bernie Lopez and I were the only two detectives left. Lopez was a new detective and somehow because of the adage of "it's who you know" was already assigned to the Homicide Unit. As I was walking around the 3rd floor, I heard a noise coming from one of the holding cells in the Assault Unit. The room was on the opposite end of the building from the Homicide Unit. Alejandro Perez was in his early twenties. Det. Lopez and I along with a Deputy DA began to interview Perez. It didn't take long, and we felt this was "the guy". As time went on, he began to crack and eventually confessed. Detective Lopez took the suspect and placed him in a room right next to the Homicide Unit un-handcuffed. Lopez thought the room was a holding cell. Oops! Not a holding cell but an unlocked interview room.

I looked up a short time later and saw Lopez with a look of terror as he said, "he's gone". My heart dropped, I felt sick. I yelled at Lopez to go one way down the hall, and I went the other. We ran down the three flights of stairs looking for the suspect. There was another detective that was still there also looking. I got to the first floor and asked the desk officer if anyone had just gone out the door. He said, "yea a Hispanic male in a white "t" shirt." That's him!!!!! I yelled at the other Detective to get on the radio and tell dispatch that the guy was outside. I ran across the cement front of the building past the city jail and parking lot. I looked down 14th St. No sign of the guy. There was a car coming at me and I stepped in front of it and told them to stop. I told them I needed their car. The driver got out. I really don't know what would have happened if I had taken his car because I had only seen that in the movies. Thank God a uniform marked car was screaming down the street and picked me up instead. It was District 6 uniform Sergeant Tony Foster. We started to search for the suspect. We were about two blocks away going the wrong way down Tremont Street. I saw the suspect run up a flight of stairs leading to a building. We aired our location and could hear sirens coming from all over. Sgt Foster ran up the stairs and around the corner to another flight of stairs. I saw that the suspect could double back and jump the wall. I slowed up a bit and watched. As I also reached the corner of the stairs, the suspect jumped Sgt Foster and grabbed his 9mm Sig Sauer pistol. I also grabbed the pistol, and the fight was on. Seemed like it was forever. Tony held back the slide, and I was able to dump the clip. We eventually got him handcuffed and put into custody.

A few days later the Lieutenant called me into his office and asked me how this guy got loose. I told him the whole story. Instead of being upset at the detective that put him in the interview room he ridiculed me for not shooting the kid. After fighting for our lives, I was very angry at what was being said and told the Lieutenant "I choose who I shoot".

This case had a real spiritual bent. Several years before this murder happened, Stephanie and I were ministering in a church. We had a long line of people that had come up for prayer. There was a lady in the line that suddenly screamed and tried to hit Stephanie with both fists. Stephanie grabbed her arms and began to pray against a spirit of death. The spirit left, and she calmed down and told us that she had been seeing herself in a coffin all week. The spirit stopped oppressing the woman and she had peace.

Months later I went to court on this case. I walked toward the court room and saw this same lady sitting on a bench near the courtroom. It turns out that the victim in this shooting was her son. The spirit of death attacked her then using the killer's vessel killed her son then almost killed me and Tony Foster in that staircase.

It reminded us that the devil comes as a roaring lion to see kill and destroy. 1 Peter 5:8 Be sober, be vigilant; because your adversary the devil, as a roaring lion, walketh about, seeking whom he may devour.

I had another unsolved homicide that I had been working on during this time frame. About 6 months earlier a girl was killed in a park in east Denver. The witnesses said that she was hit by an older Cadillac, the kind with a funny trunk. She was walking with her boyfriend in the park when the car jumped the curb, came into the park and hit her. Obviously trying to hit both of them or just one of them. I knew that was most likely an early 1980 model. A vehicle like the description was stolen that same night from about 5 blocks away. We put a hold on the vehicle for when it was recovered. About three days later the stolen vehicle was found in a parking lot near Colfax Ave. The vehicle had a broken windshield and damage to the front bumper and grill. The vehicle was towed into the police garage. The crime lab guys, and I examined the vehicle. We took measurement of all the small damage to the front of the vehicle. We also found grass stuck under the vehicle. We collected the grass. I had the crime lab take samples back at the park around where the Homicide occurred.

Our new Sergeant had been on the job about 3 years longer than I. Most of his career had been working in traffic investigations. He came into the unit with a real "I know more than you" attitude. Not good in an environment of Homicide Detectives that know, we know more than you. None of us were happy. He refused to believe this was the car that killed the girl. He kept trying to get me to release the vehicle. The crime lab even said that as far as they could tell the grass seemed to match. The lab said we should send it to a special lab that could verify it. I even had a diagram matching the injuries of the victim to the vehicle.

One night we were working a police shooting, and I ran into the new Division Chief of Investigations, who was buddies with the new Sergeant. He asked me about the car. He said so "I hear you have the wrong car on that homicide". And of course, I with no candor said, "it's the right car" and explained why.

As far as the Division Chief was concerned, I had known him my whole career. I thought we were sort of friends. But I heard he was not happy with me either. He had watched an interview I did with a city worker that had shot and killed his boss. We had interviewed this guy for over eight hours, and he finally flunked a polygraph. The Division Chief and the other Homicide Sergeant, Jon Priest, were watching me talk to the suspect again through the one-way glass in the video room. Priest knew I would get the confession and as he tells it he told the Division Chief "watch this". I stood up and went over the suspect and put my arm around his and said, "hey

I get it I work for a bunch of A-holes too". Priest told me the Chief said, "I don't like that." The guy confessed so oh well.

Chapter Twenty -Whirlwind

I could feel the tension growing in the unit. I drove into the parking lot as I got to work. As I walked towards the elevator there were two Crime Lab technicians getting their van ready to go onto the street. We said hellos and then they stopped me. "What happened?" one of the guys said. I answered, "what do you mean?". Why did you get kicked out of Homicide? My heart started beating very hard, I felt like I could not breathe. I got hot and turned red. "What are you talking about I said?" "You mean you don't even know? The whole building knows! No one can believe it. I got upstairs as fast as I could and stormed into the Sergeants office. This was Sergeant Mike Fetrow who was the night shift sergeant for Crime Against Persons. I asked him if he knew what was going on. He said, "Do you mean to tell me no one has talked to you?" He said you better call your Sergeant at home, which I did. I felt it was cowardly to only tell me to call the Lieutenant. I called the Lieutenant as you could tell he was not happy and said he would be at HQ soon. He was very angry. Not sure if he was angry at me or the Sergeant for making him handle this since he had to leave an off-duty job.

We went into his office and shut the door. I was so angry I cannot even describe it. The Lieutenant started to go down a list of things that supposedly I had done over several months. None of which I had anything to do with. His answer was only "well maybe you're getting blamed for something's you didn't do". That was it, I was out and there was no arguing the point. I asked him, "so is this a way to control everyone? If you can kick out the guys with the best record you can kick anyone out?" This guy had little Army men on his desk. I was so upset I was pounding on his desk and the men were marching around. For the next two years I never gave up asking to go back. I had asked Please don't put me in Domestic Violence. They put me in the Assault Unit for two months than you guessed it, Domestic Violence. So, after 20 years of having a favored career suddenly I felt like a slug. Made no sense to me. I was devastated. I wanted to retire from the Homicide Unit when I had my time in. I had many cases I was still working on. I had to wrap them all up and take them down to the Homicide room. No one wanted to work on them and of course the command didn't give them to anyone else because they did not care. As Joe Friday said, "Just the Facts".

      One thing I really regret is that I allowed pride to enter my life. Stephanie and I were very busy in ministry and God was working in our lives. Although obviously working Homicide was very time consuming it worked out that I just took more on call for guys so I could do ministry. I was able to take my vacations to do overseas trips and still had the highest clearance rate in the unit. We were leading a ministry leadership meeting and were on our way home. This was before things started getting bad in the unit. Stephanie told me that I was getting prideful. She said I was starting to operate in a spirit of pride. She was right. I had started to think my clearance rate was because I was such a great detective. I forgot God was giving me the wisdom. I really started to have an identity crisis and started feeling sorry for myself when I got kicked out of homicide. I felt very bad that I was not being a good example to my wife and children. I started seeing friends even people in ministry not respecting me anymore. People pulled away from Stephanie and I. Wow what a wake-up call.

I was not even allowed to be the advisory witness in the Gail Garcia Herrera case. The DAs were afraid it would come up that I had gotten kicked out of Homicide. That was a blow for sure after 12 years of work. My ego was crushed. I was not acting like the mighty man of God I thought I was.

During the trail of Charlie Wilson, I went up to testify and Charlie called me a "fat f__k" and flipped me off. That was like a commendation. Unfortunately, he did the same to the two children of Gail, now adults. How evil is that.

He was convicted of 1st Degree Murder and died in prison over 20 years later.

As I thought about what I went through I realized why it was so confusing. The previous Division Chief for Investigation had nominated me for Top Cop for the Gail Garcia Herrera case. After I got kicked out of Homicide, I received the Medal of Valor along with Sgt. Foster for capturing Perez who escaped from HQ. How does this all add up?

So, was I wronged? Yes. But how was I going to handle this. I was not emotionally handling things in a Godly way. It took several years of prayer and encouragement from Stephanie to get over this emotional rollercoaster. I realize once again that my identity is in

Christ. Being a Homicide Detective was not my identity. My identity is being a Son of God, a son, husband, father and grandfather.

I always said that the only thing better than catching a killer was saving a marriage.

One of the purposes of this book is to get people to understand that God loves them and cares about their needs. The Blood of Jesus is a powerful warfare weapon. In this book you saw the truth of Jesus blood as well as victims blood crying out for justice. You experienced Gods protection and answers.

Not long-ago Stephanie and I were ministering about marriage in a local church. Turns out that Gary Garcia, Gails brother went to that church. We spoke with him and met his wife. Our conversation with them showed us again how important family is and how much Gary loved his sister. God allows us to cross paths with people to remind us of his love. So, we can hold up each other's arms and help each other forgive.

Romans 8:34 Who is he that condemneth? It is Christ that died, yea rather, that is risen again, who is even at the right hand of God, who also maketh intercession for us.

1 John 2:1 My little children, these things write I unto you, that ye sin not. And if any man sin, we have an advocate with the Father, Jesus Christ the righteous:

Hebrews 7:25 Therefore He is also able to save to the uttermost those who come to God through Him, since He always lives to make intercession for them.

Hebrews 9:23 It was therefore necessary that the patterns of things in the heavens should be purified with these; but the heavenly things themselves with better sacrifices than these.

Jesus' blood pays it all. When the enemy sees a Christian all he can see is the blood of Christ that has been shed for the forgiveness of our sins. At the darkest time His blood shines the brightest. Just as in luminol the blood shines in the darkness. His blood is for you. He makes intersession for you. Jesus' blood is innocent and is more than a blood sacrifice that was required by Abel for atonement of sin.

Hebrews 12:24 And to Jesus the mediator of the new covenant, and to the blood of sprinkling, that speaketh better things than that of Abel.

Genesis 4 And Adam knew Eve his wife; and she conceived, and bare Cain, and said, I have gotten a man from the Lord. [2] And she again bare his brother Abel. And Abel was a keeper of sheep, but Cain was a tiller of the ground.[3] And in process of time it came to pass, that Cain brought of the fruit of the ground an offering unto the Lord.[4] And Abel, he also brought of the firstlings of his flock and of the fat thereof. And the Lord had respect unto Abel and to his offering:[5] But unto Cain and to his offering he had not respect. And Cain was very wroth, and his countenance fell.[6] And the Lord said unto Cain, why art thou wroth? and why is thy countenance fallen?[7] If thou doest well, shalt thou not be accepted? and if thou doest not well, sin lieth at the door. And unto thee shall be his desire, and thou shalt rule over him.[8] And Cain talked with Abel his brother: and it came to pass, when they were in the field, that Cain rose up against Abel his brother, and slew him.[9] And the Lord said unto Cain, Where is Abel thy brother? And he said, I know not: Am I my brother's keeper?[10] And he said, what hast thou done? the voice of thy brother's blood cried unto me from the ground.[11] And now art thou cursed from the earth, which hath opened her mouth to receive thy brother's blood from thy hand;

I felt a little like I was just talking about sour grapes in the last couple of chapters. Was I trying to justify things that happened to me? I realized my point was to be real and transparent about a dark part of my life. I really had to depend on God more than ever. The enemy was trying not only to steal my life but take my marriage and ministry. Stephanie and I had to encourage one another through this time. I thank God for her. She did not give up on me. She always told me the truth.

I really had to live:

Revelations 12:11 "[11] And they overcame him by the blood of the Lamb, and by the word of their testimony; and they loved not their lives unto the death."

I didn't know how much my job reputation meant to me. How it was overshadowing my relationship with the father. Now I do. All I can do is thank Jesus and pray this book helps someone find the Lord.

You have seen from these experiences in this book that God is real, and He loves and cares for us. He wants a personal relationship with all of us. Accept Him now as your Lord and Savior.

Stephanie and I founded a worldwide ministry called "Missionaries2Marriages". God has always had His plan for us.

Please contact us for further resources or help in your marriage

MISSIONARIES 2 MARRIAGES

PO BOX 7832
Broomfield, Colorado 80021
Office: 303-465-0342
Cell: 720-351-6211

info@missionaries2marriages.com
www.missionaries2marriages.com

Also look for us on Facebook and You Tube through our website
You can also give to our ministry on our website. We would appreciate your gift and as you partner with us you will be touching couples and families throughout the world. We are a 501C3 ministry and your gifts are tax deductible.

2 Corinthians 8:23 (CJB) As for Titus, he is my partner who works with me on your behalf; and the other brothers with him are emissaries of the congregations and bring honor to the Messiah.

Please write us at info@Missionaries2Marriages.com if you would like to be put on our email list

Here are some other resources written by Joe and Stephanie.

Fan the Flame of Your Heart Manual

This syllabus can be taught over a short time and used as a handout for a one-night event or an all-day marriage seminar. The sections include the Condition of your Heart, Covenant Love, and Discovering Oneness.

Redemption Booklet

In this booklet, Joe and Stephanie DeMott tell the story of their own testimony and how God healed their marriage.

Our "8 Keys to Breakthrough-Victory in your marriage" course is available on video and as a group study.

Printed in the USA
CPSIA information can be obtained
at www.ICGtesting.com
LVHW041357261024
794888LV00001B/75